When a Child Has Been Abused

This important and wide-ranging book explores the world of a child or young person who has been abused or neglected. It seeks to understand their world, to ease the pain from which they suffer, and to heal the wounds that the abuse has left.

Examining how abuse always takes place in the context of relationships, and involves a misuse of power that causes a traumatic overwhelming of the child or adolescent, abuse also evokes strong *countertransference*. This affects interventions, particularly when clinicians struggle with feelings of which they may feel ashamed. A difficulty in coming to terms with and addressing child abuse relates to *unconscious factors* which, by freezing the emotional area surrounding the abuse (or by blinding the area of personality), makes some thoughts unthinkable.

Considering traditional and novel ways of helping children who feel they have been maltreated, the book offers suggestions for individual treatment as well as describing the successful work carried out with child refugees. It also offers a glimpse into what child psychoanalysts interpret and do with children who feel a parent hates them.

Frances Thomson-Salo is Associate Professor and Consultant Infant Mental Health Clinician in the Centre for Women's Mental Health at the Royal Women's Hospital, Melbourne, Australia, Honorary Principal Fellow in the University of Melbourne's Department of Psychiatry, and Instructor in the University of Melbourne Graduate Diploma/Masters in Infant and Parent Mental Health, Australia.

Laura Tognoli Pasquali is a member of the International Psychoanalytical Association's Committee on Women and Psychoanalysis and former training and supervising analyst in the Italian Psychoanalytical Society.

Psychoanalysis and Women Series
Series Editor: Frances Thomson-Salo

Homosexualities: Psychogenesis, Polymorphism, and Countertransference
Edited by Elda Abrevaya, Frances Thomson-Salo

Myths of Mighty Women:
Their Application in Psychoanalytic Psychotherapy
Edited by Arlene Kramer Richards, Lucille Spira

Medea:
Myth and Unconscious Fantasy
Edited by Esa Roos

The Status of Women:
Violence, Identity, and Activism
Edited by Vivian B. Pender

Changing Sexualities and Parental Functions in the Twenty-First Century:
Changing Sexualities, Changing Parental Functions
Candida Se Holovko, Frances Thomson-Salo

The Courage to Fight Violence Against Women:
Psychoanalytic and Multidisciplinary Perspectives
Edited by Paula L. Ellman, Nancy R. Goodman

When a Child is Abused:
Towards Psychoanalytic Understanding and Therapy
Edited by Frances Thomson-Salo, Laura Tognoli Pasquali

For more information about this series, please visit: https://www.routledge.com/Psychoanalysis-and-Women-Series/book-series/KARNACPWS

When a Child Has Been Abused

Towards Psychoanalytic Understanding and Therapy

Edited by
Frances Thomson-Salo and Laura Tognoli Pasquali

LONDON AND NEW YORK

First published 2019
by Routledge
2 Park Square, Milton Park, Abingdon, Oxon OX14 4RN

and by Routledge
711 Third Avenue, New York, NY 10017

Routledge is an imprint of the Taylor & Francis Group, an informa business

© 2019 selection and editorial matter, Frances Thomson-Salo and Laura Tognoli Pasquali; individual chapters, the contributors

The right of Frances Thomson-Salo and Laura Tognoli Pasquali to be identified as the authors of the editorial material, and of the authors for their individual chapters, has been asserted in accordance with sections 77 and 78 of the Copyright, Designs and Patents Act 1988.

All rights reserved. No part of this book may be reprinted or reproduced or utilised in any form or by any electronic, mechanical, or other means, now known or hereafter invented, including photocopying and recording, or in any information storage or retrieval system, without permission in writing from the publishers.

Trademark notice: Product or corporate names may be trademarks or registered trademarks, and are used only for identification and explanation without intent to infringe.

British Library Cataloguing in Publication Data
A catalogue record for this book is available from the British Library

Library of Congress Cataloging in Publication Data
A catalog record has been requested for this book

ISBN: 978-1-138-32399-5 (hbk)
ISBN: 978-1-138-32401-5 (pbk)
ISBN: 978-0-429-45109-6 (ebk)

Typeset in Bembo
by Taylor & Francis Books

Printed and bound in Great Britain by
TJ International Ltd, Padstow, Cornwall

Contents

About the editors and contributors vii
Acknowledgements xii
Series editor foreword xiii

Introduction 1
FRANCES THOMSON-SALO

PART I
Mainly clinical 7

1 A comprehensive approach to child abuse 9
  JORDI SALA

2 Discussion of Jordi Sala's paper 18
  IRMA BRENMAN PICK

3 Child abuse as confusion of tongues 22
  LUIS JORGE MARTIN CABRÉ

4 Todd: The analysis of a latency-aged boy who self-harmed 28
  MALI A. MANN

5 The abused child – a sad, never-ending story: Some observations on abused children in the current refugee crisis 40
  MARIANNE LEUZINGER-BOHLEBER

6 The making of an abuser 50
  JOHN WOODS

7 The lost child 59
  LAURA TOGNOLI PASQUALI

8 When something that should happen does not: The unwelcome child and his psychic vicissitudes   69
MASSIMO VIGNA TAGLIANTI

9 May your steel be as sharp as your final no!   78
GEMMA ZONTINI

PART II
Protecting the care systems to prevent burnout   89

10 All in the same boat: The activity of the Abuse and Ill-Treatment Group   91
MARIA PIA CONTE AND STEFANO BOMARSI

11 Abused children: Reflections on the model   99
RENATA RIZZITELLI AND CAROLA DEL FAVERO

12 'I am naked, not just barehanded!'   104
MARIA NACCARI CARLIZZI

13 Abused children, caregivers, psychoanalysts – voices from the groups: Reflections on the model and its use   108
ANNA MARIA RISSO

14 What happens to pain: The evolution of the request   119
ELISA ALICE PELLERANO AND IVANA POZZOLI

15 The group is frightened and frightening   124
CHIARA NAPOLI AND ANNA MARIA RISSO

PART III
Legal aspects: Task and role of the judiciary in child abuse   129

16 Protecting the child and assessing the evidence: Task and role of the judiciary in child abuse   131
CRISTINA MAGGIA

Index   137

About the editors and contributors

Editors

Frances Thomson-Salo, Associate Professor, trained in the United Kingdom as an adult and child psychoanalyst and is a member of the British Psycho-analytical Society and of the Australian Psychoanalytical Society of which she is a past president. She is a training analyst and was overall chair of the Committee on Women and Psychoanalysis for the International Psycho-analytical Association from 2009–15. She is Series Editor for Karnac's *Psychoanalysis and Women* series and a member of the editorial board of the International Journal of Psychoanalysis.

Laura Tognoli Pasquali moved soon after her degree in medicine in Italy, her country of origin, to England where she worked as a psychiatrist in different hospitals and therapeutic communities. As her work was mainly in groups she became very interested in group dynamics, an interest she cultivated throughout her psychoanalytic career. She trained as a psychoanalyst in the British Psychoanalytical Society with the Kleinian group and in 1976 qualified as an analyst. Back in Italy, she worked mainly in private practice becoming a training and supervising analyst in the Italian Psychoanalytical Society. She has written several papers, some published, partly used for lectures in Italy, Germany and the United States. She now lives in a small fishing village where she loves growing flowers and plants. Taking care of plants has widened her love for teaching and her attention to clinical work; finding the best milieu for fragile young shoots helps thinking, reflecting and dreaming about the basic needs and desires of human beings. She enjoys her clinical work and in her analytic practice she has treated many women and thought deeply about the experiences they went through in their life. Therefore, with immense pleasure, she accepted to become a member of the Committee on Women and Psychoanalysis.

Contributors

Stefano Bomarsi is a psychiatrist and psychoanalyst and a member of the Italian Psychoanalytical Society.

Irma Brenman Pick came to London from South Africa in 1955 and trained first at the Tavistock Clinic as a child psychotherapist, then at the British Institute of Psychoanalysis as an adult and child analyst. She is now a distinguished fellow and training analyst in the British Society and a past president of the society. Her published papers include 'On adolescence', 'Working through in the countertransference' and 'Concern: spurious and real' – all in the *International Journal of Psychoanalysis*. Together with her late husband, Eric Brenman, she has taught extensively abroad.

Luis Jorge Martin Cabré is a full member and training and supervising analyst of the Psychoanalytic Association of Madrid (APM) and a training and supervising analyst in child and adolescent psychoanalysis. He is a member of the Spanish Society of Psychiatry and Psychotherapy for Children and Adolescents, a member of the Institute for the Study of Psychosomatic Medicine and a corresponding member of the Association Internationale d'Histoire de la Psychanalyse. He is a founding member of the International Sándor Ferenczi Foundation. He is a member of the European editorial board of the *International Journal of Psychoanalysis*. He was a member of the executive board of APM in 1991–95 and a member of the editorial board of the *Revista de Psicoanálisis de la APM* in 1994–98.

Maria Pia Conte, psychiatrist and psychoanalyst, is a full member of the Italian Psychoanalytical Society and guest member of the British Psychoanalytical Society. She is a member of OPUS and Il Nodo Group.

Carola Del Favero is a psychologist and psychotherapist and a candidate of the Italian Psychoanalytical Society. She is a member of the group, Psicoterapia e Scienze Umane. She leads clinical training groups at the Centro Psicoanalitico di Genova and at the Ruolo Terapeutico Psychotherapy Training School in Genoa. She works in private practice with adults and children, and with kindergartens as a trainer, consultant and supervisor.

Marianne Leuzinger-Bohleber is a full professor for psychoanalysis at the University of Kassel and head director of the Sigmund-Freud-Institut, Frankfurt, training analyst of the German Psychoanalytical Association and member of the Swiss Psychoanalytical Association. Her main research fields include clinical and extra clinical research in psychoanalysis, developmental research and the interdisciplinary dialogue between psychoanalysis and embodied cognitive science, educational sciences and German literature. She was awarded the Sigourney Award in 2016.

Cristina Maggia gained a law degree at Milan University in 1978. She started working as a lawyer in a famous law firm and then in 1981 she became a judge, working at the Milan Criminal Court dealing with investigations into organised crime cases until 1993, when she moved to Genoa. Here she became a judge at the Genoa Juvenile Court. Since 2012 she has been Chief of the Genoa Juvenile Prosecutor Office. In November

2014, she was elected vice president of the Italian Association of Juvenile and Family Court Judges.

Mali A. Mann is Faculty, Training and Supervising Psychoanalyst and a child supervisor at San Francisco Center for Psychoanalysis. She is the North American co-chair of the Committee on Child and Adolescent Psychoanalysis/International Psychoanalytic Association and the chair of the Inter-Committee on Child Abuse and Prevention/International Psychoanalytic Association. She is Clinical Professor, Adjunct, Department of Psychiatry and Behavioral Sciences, Stanford University Medical Center as well as the vice chair of the Adjunct Clinical Council and a faculty lecturer at the Department of Psychiatry, Child Psychiatry Division of Stanford University. She gives psychoanalytic courses and talks in the Bay Area. Mann has authored several psychoanalytic papers, book reviews, book chapters and poetry. Her book on *Psychoanalytic Aspects of Assisted Reproductive Technology* was published by Karnac. The book received the Pinnacle Book Achievement Award and the International Book Award and was a finalist in the 2016 Bookvana Awards. Her creative writing is primarily poetry and non-fiction. She has been a member of Pegasus Physician Writers since 2013. She is currently working on a collection of her poems and finds the interconnection between poetry and painting inspiring. Her artistic creative introspection is expressed through her painting. A member of the Flying Doctors for the last 20 years, she volunteers to help staff at orphanages in Mexico and treat patients in the clinics.

Maria Naccari Carlizzi, child psychiatrist and psychoanalyst, full member and expert in children and adolescents of the Italian Society of Psychoanalysis and International Psychoanalytical Association, is Adjunct Professor of Infant and Adolescent Neuropsychiatry at Genoa University. She consults to the civil and criminal courts of Genoa in family matters, abuse and ill treatment. She works in private practice with children, adolescents, adults and couples and leads work discussion groups with healthcare professionals. She is interested in combining clinical work with research, being deeply involved with the emotional development of the child, the adolescent and the couple.

Chiara Napoli is a psychiatrist and psychoanalyst working in Naples.

Elisa Alice Pellerano was born in Genoa in 1974, graduated in psychology and specialised in clinical psychology. From 2002, she worked as a psychologist and psychotherapist in private practice in Genoa. She also worked on a project to help prisoners in Genoa offering them group work as an instrument of support. She later worked as a psychotherapist in a mental health and addiction centre. She also worked in hospital training to prevent burn out, in both children and adult hospital care givers, using the group setting. In 2017, she became a member of the Italian Psychoanalytic Society and the International Psychoanalytical Association.

Ivana Pozzoli graduated in medicine in 1972, and received her PhD in psychiatry in 1977. In 1974, she started working with young psychotic and mentally disabled patients, who spent each day with carers, nurses and psychologists in an open community. She then worked in the young people's section at the psychiatric hospital in Cogoleto, Genoa. In 1979, she moved to the psychiatric hospital in Quarto, Genoa as deputy head in an adult section. In 1981, she had the opportunity to work outside the hospital environment and moved to practice in the public psychiatric service. She worked there for 13 years, with responsibility for one of the two work groups and she also founded a day hospital service for young psychotic patients and led therapeutic groups for a number of years. In 1993, she left her work in the public sector and began working as a psychoanalyst in private practice. Since 2011 she has been a full member of the Italian Psychoanalytical Society and the International Psychoanalytic Association.

Anna Maria Risso is a psychiatrist and psychoanalyst, a full member of the Italian Psychoanalytical Society and a former professor of clinical psychology at Genoa University. She has been very active in teaching in the medical school and in the psychiatric department and has taught obstetricians, paediatricians and nurses and in the school of medical oncology. She has published numerous papers in major Italian journals of psychiatry and psychoanalytic psychotherapy about group functioning and primitive mental functioning. She has been a lecturer, chair and discussant at major national and international conferences and has been the president of the Genoa Psychoanalytic Centre.

Renata Rizzitelli is a psychologist, psychotherapist and full member and expert in child and adolescent analysis of the Italian Psychoanalytical Society. She works in Genoa in private practice with children, adolescents, adults and couples. She consults in the civil court in family matters and the criminal court in investigations with victims of mistreatment and abuse. In accordance with the University of Genoa, she has designed and organises workshops held by psychoanalysts of the Genoese Centre for Psychoanalysis for the students of the course in psychology. She has also been undertaking analysis in recent years. She has worked for many years as a consultant in both the civil court, for lawsuits in legal separation, and the criminal court, and for investigating damage sustained by the victims of mistreatment and abuse.

Jordi Sala is a training analyst of the Spanish Psychoanalytical Society, working in private practice and also in a public mental health service for children and adolescents in Barcelona. He is a former general editor of the *European Psychoanalytical Federation Bulletin* (2004–2008) and is former editor of the *Catalan review of psychoanalysis (2004–2014)* and of *Focal psychoanalytic psychotherapy with children* (2009).

Massimo Vigna Taglianti is MD and Child Neuropsychiatrist. He is a full member of the Italian Psychoanalytical Society and International

Psychoanalytical Association, training and supervising analyst and scientific chair of the Italian Psychoanalytic Society. He is an adjunct professor of child and adult psychiatry at Aosta University and he also works as a psychoanalyst with children, adolescents and adults in his private practice. He is particularly interested in clinical work and in writing about transference/countertransference dynamics and above all role-reversal phenomena, as well as in the meaning of actions and play in psychoanalysis.

John Woods is a psychotherapist working in London.

Gemma Zontini is a psychiatrist and psychoanalyst working in Naples.

Acknowledgements

We acknowledge the permission given by patients to use their material, either suitably de-identified or in composite vignettes.

We thank the *Journal of Child Psychotherapy* for permission to reproduce the paper by John Woods (2016), *Journal of Child Psychotherapy*, 42 (3): 318–27.

We also thank the International Psychoanalytical Association for their ongoing commitment to the work of the Committee on Women and Psychoanalysis, our publishers, Karnac, and the authors who contributed so generously to this volume.

Series editor foreword

Frances Thomson-Salo

I am pleased, as the former overall chair of the International Psychoanalytical Association's (IPA) Committee on Women and Psychoanalysis (COWAP), for this book to be included in the growing library of the Karnac series *Psychoanalysis and Women*, which presents revisions to current understandings. Otto Kernberg, when he was president of the IPA, established COWAP in 1998 to provide a framework for the exploration of topics related to issues primarily about women, with Joan Raphael-Leff as the foundational overall chair. A hallmark of COWAP is always having been interested in engaging with other organisations and ideas, and opening a reciprocal discussion. In 2001, the mandate shifted to exploring the relations between women and men and now gender more widely.

This book is based on a conference in 2016 on the abused child held in Nervi, near Genoa, birthplace in antiquity of a venerable culture which has inspired the lives of so many over the centuries, and the presenters have furthered the debate in a way that will be felt to be respectful. The chapters offer a depth and breadth of creative and scientific interest. The writing is often poignantly evocative and powerful, and as psychoanalytic thinking and work become more complex, our understanding of the analytic process is deepened, with a greater awareness in understanding the field, which we hope in turn will lead to a new therapeutic synthesis.

Thanks to my fellow organiser without whom this conference would not have taken place nor this book resulted – Laura Tognoli Pasquali, who when I asked probably slightly less than a year previously if she would like to take up the challenge hardly hesitated before saying yes.

Lastly, we thank the IPA for their ongoing commitment to the work of the COWAP and, in particular, Stefano Bolognini, for the unwavering support of the IPA.

Introduction

Frances Thomson-Salo

I trained, as did Laura Tognoli Pasquali, with the British Psychoanalytical Society, and we are now collaborating to try to ameliorate the pain of solitude and shame of the child who has been abused, to give words to what often feels unspeakable, in a contribution of the International Psychoanalytical Society towards understanding and relieving suffering worldwide. We acknowledge the debt we owe to many before us who have brought their understanding to bear on such children (Heineman, 1998).

We thank the authors who have allowed us the privilege of sharing their work in such difficult situations with thoughtful papers that aid us to begin thinking about how to help all concerned – children, parents and families, therapists and societies as well as those who abuse, who are sometimes indistinguishable from those who have been abused, as they attempt to get on with living their lives.

We are concerned to deepen understanding of how someone comes to abuse another, how one may begin a short-term intervention to underpin a longer-term process and how to support the wider system of family and other systems. We seek answers to understand those for whom culture's best guidance has not been able to help them structure their lives, so that children need less often to feel deserted in solitude and pain. We hope to increase our understanding of how to help meet these needs and support children and young people as a population of vulnerable children have experienced maltreatment in their lives. When a light is shone on abuse it allows other examples of abuse to come into the light and to this effort the International Psychoanalytical Association (IPA) wishes to contribute psychoanalytic understanding, and hopes that these papers will contribute further understanding.

In 2015, as the chair of the Committee of Women and Psychoanalysis (COWAP), I implemented an inter-committee project on the prevention of child abuse, and at the Boston IPA Congress the following six chairs and their committees set aside a day on 21 July 2015 to work on definitions and interventions: Child and Adolescent Psychoanalysis, Psychoanalysis and Law Committee, World Health Organization Committee, the United Nations Committee, Psychoanalytic Perspectives of Family and Couples and COWAP. This conference from which the papers in this book are drawn was planned before the inter-committee was set up and we are very hopeful that we continue to work together in the future. I quote below from the minutes prepared by Kerry Kelly Novick at the Boston IPA Congress Inter-Committee Day on Child Abuse (21 July 2015):

> Relevant psychoanalytic ideas are that
> - Abuse is *inter-generational*.
> - Abuse is often rooted in *early interactions/attachment patterns*.
> - Abuse always involves a misuse of power, leading to traumatic overwhelming – psychoanalysts can use their historical and evolving corpus of understanding about *trauma*.
> - Abuse is a *subjective, inner experience*, according to the definition of trauma as internal, whatever the source of the overwhelming.
> - Abuse always takes place in the context of *relationships*.
> - The *developmental point of view* is essential, as repercussions of abuse are long-term.
> - Abuse always implicates *infantile sexuality*, either directly or through sadomasochistic relationships, as well as when it takes a violent, aggressive form.
> - Increased knowledge of and attention to *resilience* is fruitful.
> - The developmental *phase of parenthood*, defined as putting a child's needs and best interests first, is directly relevant, given that abuse implicates use of the child for the adult's needs instead.
> - Abuse evokes strong *countertransferences*, which affects interventions.
> - A difficulty in coming to terms with, addressing, and changing child abuse relates to the *unconscious factors that make aspects unthinkable*. Psychoanalysts know about the unconscious.
> - The *multidimensionality* of abuse relates to the basic psychoanalytic stance, in contrast to a unidimensional perspective.
>
> Other points in the discussion included the following ones:
> - We speak always to three strands: *body, internal life, interactions with world and others*. Speaking to the *ownership of self, not just the body*, expresses greater complexity.
> - *Training* of allied professionals is crucial, to disseminate central ideas, such as infantile sexuality (broadening out from genital sexuality as the model).
> - *Parent groups* can be helpful at many levels of development.

Assessment instruments should include *projective elements*, to reach less conscious derivatives, but must be designed to be reliable and valid.

We noted that there has been an international cultural evolution of awareness in most societies of child abuse, which we see as linked to increased valuing of children. Nevertheless, there remains wide variation internationally in acknowledging and backing up the personhood of children with action, recognising their intrinsic value as individuals. We noted that increased incidence statistics are hard to interpret, as reporting rates are affected by social, attitudinal and legal changes. A general sense, however, of increased internal tension in adults in many countries, related perhaps to heightened experiences of powerlessness in the modern world, despite the paradoxical presence of increased freedom, may reflect real changes in the amount of abuse in first-world countries.

The papers in the book, although they may at first sight seem narrow, elaborate a broad range of perspectives and ideas and in that way are timely – an exploration of the implicit dynamics triggered by maltreatment and abuse; the need to distinguish types of abuse and the long-term effect of cumulative trauma; a reminder that sexuality occurs in both body and mind, and the different burdens for the child that ensue. These include having to manage feelings of guilt, unfairness, hate, shame and worthlessness contained in the existential question of 'Will I be enough if I allow myself to be abused?' as well as the role reversal of the young child who may have to some extent to act for the adult and to help them manage expressions of their sexuality. How do we help the child feel that the abuse and neglect should not have happened and to keep hope alive when often there seems so little opposing the abuse and neglect?

The chapters present many deeply felt countertransference reactions. The challenges for the therapist in experiencing, processing and sharing countertransference experiences were also elaborated, ranging from encountering repetition of the abuser/victim dynamic in having to confront the abuser in oneself and the risk of identifying with the victimhood of the child while recognising hatred and aggression as attempts to survive loss and vulnerability. As psychoanalysts, our therapeutic method permits a nearness to the victim or perpetrator that may be unique insofar as we cannot turn away from the experiences and we need to address them and try to understand them. We approach this understanding from the psychoanalytic treatment, as the countertransference, from the understanding and treatment of the perpetrator and from the often lifelong consequences for the victims and those suffering. Much of course is not covered, such as a gender analysis of adolescents or adults with a paedophilic breakdown (Wood, 2017) and against whom most of the abuse is committed (and with the collusion of others). We turn now to outline the organisation of the chapters.

Organisation of the chapters

Jordi Sala begins by laying out an overall approach to understanding child abuse, with clinical vignettes illustrating neglect and possible sexual abuse. His chapter is discussed by Irma Brenman Pick from the British Psychoanalytical Society and illustrated with a longer vignette where it seems likely that an adult patient had been abused as a child. Luis Jorge Martin Cabré discusses Ferenczi's concepts, particularly his concept of confusion of tongues, and how traumatic it is for a child not to be listened to and their experience denied; the younger the infant the more incomprehensible and confused the experience. While Jordi Sala's chapter may seem to stress the role of the mother in an unboundaried seductiveness, a theme which is picked up at various points throughout the book including by Gemma Zontini, in most of the vignettes sexual abuse if described is perpetrated by males.

The focus then turns to how to help the child who feels used and abused and the need to become more knowledgeable of different ways of helping such children. Mali Mann, who chairs the new IPA inter-committee on child abuse, gives a detailed case study of a boy who feels abandoned rather than one who is actively neglected or physically abused. Mali Mann has given this case material sacrificing extensive discussion such as, for example, how might an analyst do an assessment when a child presents in their consulting room, in order that the reader can see for themselves in an unvarnished way both child and analyst at work. This is followed by a chapter by Marianne Leuzinger-Bohleber on psychoanalytic crisis intervention work with traumatised refugees, particularly children and adolescents, many of whom are multiply physically and sexually abused during their refugee flight, and this is one of many psychoanalytically inspired initiatives to understand and help suffering children. It discusses specific challenges and treatment techniques with this group and presents current work from Germany about how to ameliorate the ongoing traumatisation for children in the current refugee crisis, in particular the very important psychoanalytic work done at the Sigmund Freud Institute with Marianne Leuzinger-Bohleber's psychoanalytic experience being carried out with children who are abused by the terrible condition of being refugees.

John Woods in his chapter examines carefully how a child may attempt to deal with the trauma of having been abused, probably sexually, by in turn becoming an abuser; there are elements of this in Laura Tognoli Pasquali's chapter where again her patient is likely to have been sexually abused as a child. These papers were felt to represent well the confused and confusing identity of the abused and the abuser. Woods' paper highlights that the analyst, too, *will* sooner or later become an abuser in the transference and *should* recognise the pain in this. In Laura Tognoli Pasquali's chapter, as well as in John Woods', only by reliving the abuse in the transference is it possible to get fully in touch with it. This leads to the question that we may pay too little attention generally to the emotional stress of our work of being seen as an abuser by those whom we are supposed to be helping. In a particularly poignant end to Tognoli Pasquali's chapter she touches on the abuse of a child who is not physically or sexually abused but does not exist for his parents and therefore for himself. Massimo Vigna Taglianti picks up this topic of the child who is not wanted by the parents, or from whom the parent turns away, and with Gemma Zontini illustrates this with material from work with adults who were neglected as children.

Marianne Leuzinger-Bohleber had referred to the strain on staff attending to the refugee children and Chapter 10 returns to this and the work that Genoese psychoanalysts are doing to reach out and provide group work opportunities to the wider care systems. Chapters 10–15 deal with protecting the care systems to prevent burnout in the staff and convey very vividly through the many voices speaking the strain that the analysts who take part in different groups in the community are under. Chapter 16 addresses legal aspects from the point of view of a judge charged with protecting the child and assessing the evidence, and although it is from the Italian model it is likely to have many points that are widely applicable.

At the same time, we are aware that we do not see directly in psychoanalysis or psychoanalytic therapy many of the worst environmental excesses so that it may be easy to sanitise child sexual abuse or the kind of abuse suffered by children affected by their environment or who are born drug affected or rapidly become drug affected (Internet References 1; 3). Their mothers seem likely to have been multiply abused in their lives, in what is likely to have been a trans-generational inheritance, and the burnout in the workers is a kind of abuse that is passed on. Anne Manne's account of the Child Abuse Commission in Australia, *Rape among the lamingtons* (2017), conveys clearly so much of the brutality so that no shirking from the horror is possible (Internet Reference 2).

Only in contact and discussion with each other from different working places and countries can we ameliorate the life of children and work on the prevention of abuse. Meeting in conferences and the sharing that ensues aids in containing the emotional burden carried.

My personal thanks to Laura Tognoli Pasquali for organising the conference. I think when you read her chapter you may agree that the young man could have sought her out knowing she could hear what the adults in his childhood had not been able to.

References

Heineman, T. V. (1998). *The Abused Child: Psychodynamic Understanding and Treatment.* New York: Guildford Press.

Wood, H. (2017). Paedophilia, or Paedophilic Breakdown? The Impetus to Seek Illegal Images Online. Presented at Psychoanalysis in the Techno-Culture Age: Challenges of the Black Mirror Conference, Melbourne Brain Centre, Parkville, Melbourne, 20 May.

Internet references

1 www.theguardian.com/us-news/2017/may/17/ohio-drugs-child-protection-workers?CMP=share_btn_link (accessed 15 May 2017).
2 www.themonthly.com.au/issue/2017/may/1493560800/anne-manne/rape-among-lamingtons (accessed16 May 2017).
3 www.amazon.co.uk/Suffer-Little-Children-Irelands-Industrial/dp/0826414478 (accessed 17 May 2017).

Part I
Mainly clinical

1 A comprehensive approach to child abuse

Jordi Sala

Not being a specialist in the field of child abuse, what I can offer you is a clinical and psychoanalytic overview of the subject, as one of many possible frameworks that might help us to approach the implicit dynamics triggered by maltreatment and abuse. We are familiar with Klein's statement that all a child needs from the outset is 'food, love and understanding' (Klein, 1946, 1959) for a mind that is more or less sane to develop. But we know this is not always what they receive.

We assume that the birth of a mind is the result of an encounter between mother and child. As we know, these first encounters in life constitute a very complex situation from which the nascent mind will gradually emerge, differentiating what belongs to them from what belongs to others. And the very first steps of this process, we assume, are made through *contact* with the mother, both corporeal and mental, thanks to which, unconnected parts of the body/mind experience with another (mother) are held together, leading to a progressively more coherent body/mind self (Bick, 1986; Gaddini, 1981; Stern, 1985), wherein boundaries are of great psychological significance. But contact with a primal object may be either more or less adequate or pernicious. Let us consider, from the outset, that maltreatment and abuse represent 'a kind of contact' with no regard for child's needs, a contact that violates the very frontiers of the body/mind self. In considering this, what inevitably springs to mind is *trauma*, with its *effects* and its *dynamics*.

Contact, thus, is a very sensitive matter since it has the power to stir sensations, to mediate emotions and phantasies and to build a relationship through which a mind is created or (might be) destroyed. Let me mention here Shengold (1992), who describes the syndrome of 'soul murder' as the deliberate attempt to interfere with the child's separate identity, joy in life and capacity to love, caused by seduction, overstimulation, cruelty, indifference or neglect. In child abuse, contact is generally used for the gratification of an adult's perverse sexual desire and/or to placate their anxieties by putting them violently into the child's body.

We presuppose, according to Bion (1962a, 1962b), that there is an inborn expectation in the baby of something good outside that will provide for their needs. When this expectation on the part of the infant is met through experience with the mother that is good, we hypothesise, this experience becomes a central part of the very nucleus of the self, and hence the core of the sane part of the personality as a whole. The self coheres around repeated and anticipated experiences with its good object. This, of course, can be described in other ways: such as, for example, that the adequate sharing, by the caregiver, of an infant's inner experiences (and expectations), leads the infant to feel known and results in increased feelings of security and attachment, protecting against feelings of alienation and aloneness (Stern, 1985).

However, in the case of violent and disruptive experiences with a bad object in reality, the infant's expectations do not meet with a (good) realisation, nor even with absence of realisation in the form of frustration/deprivation, but rather a 'counter-realisation', so to speak, of being overwhelmed. An incomprehensible intense 'something' intrudes upon the child's body/self, turning upside down the natural structure wherein the child's need for projection can be mostly contained and transformed. According to Bion (1962a), with the reversal of the containing function the 'development of an apparatus for thinking is disturbed and instead there takes place a hypertrophic development ... of an apparatus for ridding the psyche of accumulations of bad internal objects (beta elements)' (pp. 306–10).

In abuse, a child's needs and expectations are not properly met. Instead, somatosensory intrusions, of a traumatic character, non-conceptualised, non-articulated in an inner or interpersonal dialogue, are likely to produce severe damage in the structure of the self, either in the form of fragmentation, thought disturbances, affective disorders, unmanageable anxieties and the like, often promoting the use of dissociation and the hosting of an unacknowledged aggression. This is true of all victims of child abuse, whether they are a physically, emotionally or sexually abused child. Davies and Frawley (1992), from their own and others' investigations into the consequence of child abuse, confirm the recurring connection between childhood trauma, particularly physical and sexual trauma, and the process of dissociation. The authors see dissociation, in this case, as an organisation of the mind in which traumatic memories are split off from associative accessibility to conscious thought. Rather than being repressed and forgotten, they alternate in a mutually exclusive pattern with other conscious ego states. Dissociation becomes the only means to survive when the defenceless child cannot escape or fight against the abuser, as is so graphically expressed in adult terms by a very young victim of child sexual abuse: 'While I was being raped I left my body, floating out of it and up to the ceiling ... out of the room' (Rhodes, 2016, p. 28).

We assume that investing the body with meaning is of critical importance. Just to give two examples:

1   Being poorly stimulated might trigger phantasies, in the child's mind, either of not being wanted or only poorly loved, as having little or no value at all in the eyes of another.

2   In the case of a disorganised and confusing experience of contact, violence done to the body of the infant might make them believe, at one (representational) level, that they are unworthy and bad. But more disturbingly, at a deeper level it might create a violent, fragmented and disorganised mind, which might later cohere around identification with the aggressor. It is this latter scenario that I hope to illustrate later from the experience of Christian.

What I mean by these two examples is that the first meaning of a child's life comes from the interaction with his caregiver, an adult that supplies meaning to one's existence, both in body and mind. In this regard, it is worth recalling, just in passing, Laplanche's views on the *seduction theory* regarding the consequences of asymmetry between infant and caregiver, indicating that the sexual message always originates in the adult, by which we should understand that the foundational moment of the self is in the (sexual/libidinal) investment that the (m)other puts on the infant (Laplanche, 1997). But a mother/adult, we hope, is able to distinguish love and respect for the child's needs from her own sexual investment and phantasies.

But, what happens when the adult's phantasies are allowed to impinge upon the child? And what is the difference between investing in phantasies and acting them out? What kind of phantasies does the abuse trigger in the child? Here we think of various severe consequences such as confusion between adult/child, inner/outer world, phantasy/reality, with the subsequent collapse of the symbolic; but also, we find play and thinking pervaded with sexual and/or aggressive connotations; deprivation of affective needs inflicted with deception and treachery; omnipotence and promiscuity on the child's side based on triumph and rivalry in oedipal terms; and the constant presence of guilt and shame during later life. All this can be summed up by saying that child (sexual) abuse robs a child of his or her most precious properties: childhood itself, intimacy, security and trust.

> For all sexually abused children a fundamental rule has been broken. The natural role of an adult as guardian and protector has been abandoned, the stronger has exploited and damaged the weaker and the child has lost unequivocal faith in the existence of an adult world that is by and large benign and favourable to development.
>
> (Skelton, 2006)

Maltreatment of children

This is now a subject often addressed in psychoanalysis. Over the past decades, there has been agreement in differentiating between *physical, emotional* and *sexual abuse* on the one hand, and *neglect* on the other. We need adequate terms to identify a problem to begin to recognise and therefore address it appropriately. But we also need a frame of reference where the phenomenon can be contemplated. Maltreatment of children is more frequent than is generally recognised. We often take for granted, without much thought, the assumption that parents or adults are going to be caring and concerned unless they are mentally ill.

And certainly, in the case of mental illness we are more likely to be alert to the presence, and consequences, of abuse and neglect in the family, and thus able to set in motion therapeutic actions to prevent and help abused or neglected children. For in these cases,

> abused children often have to contend with a host of other difficulties as well; child disability or ill health, parental history of being a child victim of abuse, parental emotional impairment, parental substance misuse, domestic violence, poverty. This wide range of child, family, and parental adverse circumstances all interact and influence each other. [However, we must not forget that] the consequences of child abuse and child sexual abuse are equally protean, and appear to be influenced by the environment and the availability of good experiences with other parents or carers.
> (Jones & Ramchandani, 1999, cited in McQueen et al., 2015, p. 27)

But abuse and neglect often occur in silence. Young-Bruehl (2005) argues that the chief obstacle to the discovery of child abuse and neglect is precisely a shared belief that parents/adults, as such, in what we assume to be the normal population, are more likely than not to fulfil their responsibilities as parents/adults – particularly their child's expectation that they will be loved. But if this belief is taken for granted, we remain blind and deaf to abuse, overlooking certain hints that the abused child might send out to those around them in forms that are more or less disguised.

Contact and boundaries need to be considered in their particular nature: that is, taking into account the quantity, intensity and quality of the contact, whether it is excessive or defective, adequate or inappropriate, benign or malign. But if we specifically consider the abuse perpetrated on children, we also need to be attentive to: *when* it is done (precocity), *what* is done (the kind of abuse) and *by whom* (inside or outside of the family/confidence circle). The extent to which the personality will be affected depends on the particular combination in each child. And once again we find ourselves in the area of trauma.

At this point, it is pertinent to refer to Alvarez (1992), who suggests that we are more or less familiar with the possibility of working on trauma on integrative lines (where the traumatic material is recovered, thought, fantasised and dreamt about), or the alternative encapsulation of all circumstances connected to trauma. But a third and more serious possibility needs to be taken into account: namely, the situation where 'trauma influences ongoing developmental processes, such as memory, cognition, learning and, of course, personality' (p. 157). And she goes on to argue that in severe and chronically sexually abused children, we should think of a theory of forgetting as opposed to a theory of remembering, so as to enable the child to think about his trauma in tiny and manageable digestible doses. This implies having respect, in treatment, for the child's own pace: 'Maybe each single aspect of the abuse, bits and pieces of the experience, particularly if it was chronic may need to be digested one step at a time' (p. 154). In his autobiography, *Instrumental, a memoir of madness, medication and music*, James Rhodes (2016) describes very vividly how the sexual abuse he suffered from the age of 5, for five years uninterruptedly, penetrated the core of his self and remained there forever, as a stain that marked him as evil, disturbing almost every minute of his daily life, both in mind and in body, with unbearable and unavoidable symptoms that often made him think of himself as mad and unable to build a proper and caring loving relationship.

> I had sex young. It was bad. I am bad … It's one of those hideous face-blot stain things that children stare at and adults look away from. It is just there all the time and nothing I do can or will erase it. I know all the time that there is nowhere I can put it, no way I can frame or reframe it, nothing I can do with it to make it bearable or acceptable … He [the abuser] took my childhood away from me. He took my child away from me, he took fatherhood away from me.
>
> (p. 26)

Now, after the unfolding of this rough scheme on the subject of child abuse, I would like to illustrate some of the ideas put forward here with two clinical examples of my own, taken from my clinical practice in a public mental health department in Barcelona: first the case of a 5-year-old physically abused child, and then one session, approaching the end of a family psychotherapy, where child abuse of one of the family members is uncovered.

Vignette 1: Christian (a schizophrenic mother and her son's disorganised psychosis): long-term consequences

I saw Christian for the first time when he was 5 years old, and met with him weekly until he was 7 years old. At that time, a severe disorganised type of infantile psychosis was diagnosed. He was unmanageable, continuously confronting parents, teachers and children of his age, with no respect for limits, switching from warm and caring contact on the adult's lap to uncontainable physical and verbal violence if he was frustrated. The grandmother, who had custody of the child, was at her wits' end with him. In the sessions, the child could tolerate no boundaries, and spent most of the time abusively trying to gain control of me, often physically. Some months after the beginning of treatment I met his mother and some things began to fall into place: his mother was giving him contradictory orders continuously, and the child paid absolutely no attention to her. The mother chased him around my office, smacking him, shouting that he was bad and had no respect for her. It quickly became obvious that the mother was severely ill, having been diagnosed with schizophrenia. I later found out that the father, who was suffering many complications due to his obesity, was extremely passive, had learning difficulties and was totally out of touch with the world of feelings. During the child's treatment, the mother had to be hospitalised in a psychiatric ward and for some time, on weekdays, the child was looked after in a psycho-educative institution.

Eleven years later he came to our mental health department referred by the Young Court Authority. A psychotherapeutic approach was assessed. He was 18 and was visited by a colleague in our department for a short period of time, until he disappeared leaving no trace. A psychotherapeutic treatment was indicated as alternative to penal punishment. He was sent for disorderly behaviour, threats, mugging, burglary and addiction to cannabis. The professional who was dealing with him considered him unfocused, theatrical, extravagant, and wondered about the possibility of delusional activity. He was fascinated by firearms and explained how the first time he had killed a pigeon he felt remorseful, but that a little later, with a friend, he had tortured a cat to death. He asked to see me, and we exchanged words briefly in the waiting room. He said, affectionately, 'Do you remember me? I was really bad back then. I don't know how you put up with me!' In the short time that we spoke, he explained to me that he had come for therapy after being arrested for theft, and that during the intervening years he had been in the care of social services, and had been institutionalised in a centre run by the General Delegation for Child and Adolescent Care, because his grandmother was too elderly to look after him. He reminded me that his mother was ill and that he had not had news of his father for years.

The lapse of time showed how the maltreatment and neglect that Christian had suffered as a child, in a family setting characterised by mental illness, had taken their toll in the young adult. Eleven years later, his identification with the aggressor was evident in the cruelty he inflicted on animals. And just as he had done as a child of 5, he was still defying the limits (now the group and social limits set by the community), transgressing them (through robbery, antisocial behaviour, drug addiction); the limits were powerless to contain his disrupted mind, fraught with violence, incapable of finding its place in his fragmented self.

This child had grown up in an environment where the parental function of containment was not only unavailable to him, but had been turned upside down: the intense projections of his parents, the uncontrolled anxiety and hostility of the mother emptied out into this vulnerable child's mind and acted, in the course of his development, as a traumatic intrusion, severely hampering the integration of his experiences into a coherent self.

I trust that this example will serve to illustrate the extent to which child abuse has serious consequences in the short and long term, in that it often reproduces and might be passed on to the next generation: a major challenge for our social services, our educational services, our mental health care and our society as a whole as regards the attention and prevention policies that we adopt.

Vignette 2: Child sexual abuse and mental illness: Sam

At the beginning of a session in the second year of family therapy, the father asks his son to disclose what they, the parents, had discovered by chance at home, while looking at his email inbox that he had left open. Sam, the son, now 22, diagnosed with a borderline personality disorder, replies that it is of no importance except for them, his parents, being so conservative. The father insists. The son then explains that it all has to do with Ralph, a man in his 60s, whom he met at the Film Library ten years previously and is now a close friend of the family. The son had just turned 13 at the time and was already recognised as a very disturbed child. Ralph approached him in an extremely sensitive manner, they became acquainted with each other, and then little by little Ralph taught him things about life, and shared many interesting ideas about cinema. They then became close friends and met regularly. The mother asks his son to be more straightforward.

He then says: 'I know that you mean sex, it is the only thing that seems to matter to you two. Yes, we had sex.'

The father asks since when. *Were you forced to have it?*

Sam replies, 'Since the very beginning of our relationship ... yes, two or three times I was forced. Then it pleased me and I looked for further opportunities. Ralph opened my eyes to a new world, something you will never understand. Thanks to Ralph I now have an open mind, I don't mind having sex with a boy, a girl, a mature man or whoever. Sex is a far more enriching experience than that exclusive, boring and limited man to woman affair.'

His mother says, 'You say the same thing when referring to drugs, that drug taking is enriching.'

Sam: 'I have repeated many times to you that I am not a drug addict. I like drugs, I like experimenting, having new and unknown pleasurable sensations. But I am not at all dependent on any one drug.'

Father replies: 'Let's stick to what we were saying. You were raped. Now you told us that you no longer have sex with Ralph but that you are proud of that experience and that you would repeat it if the same situation arose again.'

The mother adds that they (the parents) feel so guilty. She says 'Ralph has been part of the family since that time when Sam met him, he has become a close friend to all of us, we all go together on excursions to the country, we invite him to family events as if he was the children's uncle. And, all of a sudden, unexpectedly, we find out about the sexual abuse.'

Sam defends Ralph and the experience they had. The parents confronted Ralph, who did not seem to feel guilty, ashamed or anything of the sort. On the contrary, he claimed he loved and still loves Sam. He is someone very special to him, he only wishes him well. He would never do anything to harm him.

At this point, I see that the parents are devastated, disconsolate. Sam is glancing at me surreptitiously and intermittently.

His father says: 'If you think like this about the sexual abuse, would you do the same in future with another child of your age? Do you think that is fair?'

Sam answers: 'I wouldn't force anybody, but if he asked me I would teach him. I can't see what's wrong with that.'

In a subsequent session, when the son was absent, the parents reflected, with pain, on how it has all been possible, they did not suspect anything, now that they know it makes sense for them as they look back on that period of their son's life, when he was about 14 years old, wandering around the Old Quarter of the city, at night, looking for transvestites and prostitutes with whom to have sex.

Short comments on this material

Sam leaves his letterbox open, one of the means by which his parents finally discover the secret that had been hidden from them for more than ten years. Or maybe the young man has been dropping hints that they had not been able to pick up on because such a possibility would simply never have entered their heads. They are shocked and scandalised by a discovery that caught them completely unawares. At no point did they wonder why an adult, some 40 years older, was trying to hang out with their son, and establish such a close friendship with him. Not only did they not suspect anything, but they even welcomed this man into the family, as if he were just another uncle, as they put it. Their naivety is clearly the result of dissociation and denial of their own and of their son's sexuality, and of the fantasies associated with it. These parents appear to have abdicated some of the parental responsibilities that would have served to protect their particularly vulnerable, and mentally fragile son from sexual abuse. They assumed that Ralph, being an adult with exquisite manners, could only possibly have positive intentions with regard to their son.

In the interview the parents force their son to 'confess', in front of the analyst, his secret and the 'bad things' he had been doing and hiding from them, thus displacing their own unbearable feelings of guilt for having been so blind and deaf to the sexual abuse that had been going on right in front of them. In the interview, the boy reacts to this paternal pressure by making a provocative exhibition and defence of his sexual activity with Ralph, which takes the form of intense aggression, though he does not recognise it as such, against his parents. Far from repressing his memory of the experience, forgetting that the abuse had taken place, he defends it as a right and as having been good for his personal development, just like drugs. Due to the use of denial and split neither Sam nor his parents are capable of connecting these traumatic events with, or considering the role they might have played in, the disorders of thinking, relationship and behaviour that characterise him, and which make everyday life with him so unbearable.

Conclusion

We see how secrecy has prevailed concerning sexual abuse for many years: how the abuser has apparently no idea of the damage caused, how the abused might identify with and defend the abuser as somebody who brought good into his life, how neither the abuser nor the abused seem not to feel guilt and/or shame, but the parents, for their screening out and denial of ongoing abuse which could have been detected and treated much earlier. To conclude, my intention has been to approach the topic in terms that might be of some use, as one of the possible frameworks for the discussion of such a difficult and painful phenomenon.

References

Alvarez, A. (1992). Child sexual abuse: the need to remember and the need to forget. In *Live Company*. London and New York: Routledge.
Bick, E. (1986). Further considerations on the function of the skin in early object relations: findings from infant observation integrated into child and adult analysis. *British Journal of Psychotherapy*, 2: 292–299.
Bion, W. (1962a). A theory of thinking. *International Journal of Psycho-analysis*, 43: 306–310; republished (1967) in *Second Thoughts*. London: William Heinemann Medical Books, pp. 110–119.
Bion, W. (1962b). *Learning from Experience*. London: Heinemann.
Davies, J. M. & Frawley, M. G. (1992). Dissociative processes and transference-countertransference paradigms in the psychoanalytically oriented treatment of adult survivors of childhood sexual abuse. *Psychoanalytic Dialogues*, 2: 5–36.
Gaddini, E. (1981). Note sul problema mente-corpo. *Rivista di Psicoanalisi*, 27: 3–29.
Klein, M. (1946). Notes on some schizoid mechanisms. In *CWMK*, Vol III. London: Hogarth Press.
Klein, M. (1959). Our adult world and its roots in infancy. In *CWMK*, Vol III. London: Hogarth Press.
Laplanche, J. (1997). The theory of seduction and the problem of the other. *International Journal of Psycho-analysis*, 78: 653–666.
McQueen, D., Itzin, C., Kennedy, R., Sinason, V. & Maxted, F. (2015). *Psychoanalytic Psychotherapy after Child Abuse*. London: Karnac.
Rhodes, J. (2016). *Instrumental: A Memoir of Madness, Medication and Music*. London: Cannongate Books.
Shengold, L. (1992). Child abuse and treatment examined. *Bulletin of the Anna Freud Centre*, 15: 189–204.
Skelton, R. (Ed.) (2006). *The Edinburgh International Encyclopaedia of Psychoanalysis*. Edinburgh: Edinburgh University Press. Entry: sexually abused children (psychotherapy with).
Stern, D. N. (1985). *The Interpersonal World of the Infant*. New York: Basic Books.
Young-Bruehl, E. (2005). Discovering child abuse. *Scientific Meeting of the American Institute For Psychoanalysis: American Journal of Psychoanalysis*, 65: 293–295.

2 Discussion of Jordi Sala's paper

Irma Brenman Pick

Like, everyone I imagine, I am most grateful to Jordi for his rich and stimulating paper. It is an account so comprehensive that I have not found it easy to think about what I might add to the discussion. But perhaps I might use this opportunity to address just a few of the points he has made. He writes, that in child abuse, contact is generally used for the gratification of an adult's perverse sexual desire, and/or to placate their anxieties by putting them violently into the child's body. He goes on to speak of the child becoming overwhelmed.

I would like to add that as well as for purposes of sexual gratification, and projection of anxiety, as Jordi Sala so vividly conveys, children may be abused in other ways; parental depression, for example, may be cruelly projected from early on, in a way that may also be damaging. A 5-year-old boy, Petr, whose parents are intensely anxious about any difficulty he might show, draws a truck in his session. He tells the therapist that this is a baby truck. He then draws different vehicles piled upon the truck and tells her that these are all broken-down cars, scooters, bikes and so on, and that the poor baby truck has to carry all these broken-down things. He continues, saying that he has to get them fixed; he is not going to the dump with them but to a garage. He then says that it is all too much for the baby truck and he has to do something about this, get some help. Then he draws a bigger truck, which he tells her is the Daddy truck. He says that he will now transfer all the broken-down cars, scooters and so on onto the Daddy truck, and Daddy will have to get it fixed.

So, while there is some hope of a father who will deal with these problems, he also seems to communicate an experience of having to bear too great a burden in relation to parental difficulties which are projected onto him, that is, which he needs to carry.

In a very moving paper, Donald Moss gives an account of how such feelings may be passed on. He describes how as a young man, when he had arrived late (for reasons beyond his control) for his beloved grandfather's funeral, his aunt, angry with him for missing the funeral, slapped him on the face. Many years later he saw in consultation a patient who complained about him (the analyst) holding his hand in front of his face; by their third meeting the patient rose from his chair and shouted: 'Take your fucking hand off your fucking face.'

He, the analyst, was afraid that the patient would smash his face in; he was able to get the patient to leave, but also felt humiliated by his fear, experiencing himself as a weakling. Going down to the Underground later, he saw a stunted homosexual man on the platform – and felt a sudden urge to smash his face in! Identifying then with being the big one smashing the other, rather than the weakling being smashed.

So, we see how the feelings stirred up within, caused him to wish violently to attack a vulnerable person who has done him no harm; he wishes to rid himself of the shame of being 'weak'. In this way, as Jordi Sala writes, persons who cannot manage their own painful feelings may use the infant, or child, and I would add, or patient, or vulnerable other, as a containing object. In a different context, Christoph Hering, writing about the film *The Alien* (1994), shows how such films, rather than helping the audience to work through such fears, instead excite the audience. The small boy of whom I spoke above knew that he needed a father to help him deal with his overwhelmed feelings. When instead the father (or film director) excites him further, the feelings become seriously unmanageable. And of course, all this is not far removed from the current theatre of political rhetoric.

I would like now to return to the specific question of child sexual abuse, and think about what it is about sexual abuse that makes it so damaging. I have in mind a clinical example, which I think is fairly typical of those who have suffered abuse: the patient is a young (abused) Jewish woman, now in her 30s; for a long time, she has had repeated phases 'where I don't feel well at all, where I have problems with everything: all the important areas in my life, my studies, work, the relationship to my boyfriend and my family'. When this happens, she is not able to cope with the simplest things, then she cannot manage anything.

Her severe anxieties could reach panic levels: shortly after starting analysis, she developed the fear that her analyst *might* attack her aggressively while she was in the waiting room or on the toilet. These extremely threatening fantasies finally became so frightening for the patient that she tried first through self-mutilation (cutting her arm), later through thoughts of suicide (taking sleeping tablets and then getting drunk in the bath with the intention of drowning), to get some relief from this extreme fear. At this point in the treatment, the analyst changed the setting and continued treating the patient in the sitting position.

The patient's *father* is described as often quick-tempered and also violent. She tried to keep out of his way as often as possible. There is also evidence to suggest that he sexually abused her. Her *mother* the patient depicts as being a very dependent and also a needy person who makes totally unreasonable demands on her daughter to support her (the mother), and then denies this. 'This (denial) drives me crazy.'

She has had a boyfriend for some years who was addicted to marihuana; this was a cause of conflict, for he then totally neglected her needs. When she separated from him she was at times overwhelmed with panic 'that *something will happen to me*, I will be attacked by someone', and she then felt threatened that *her analyst might* physically attack her. I think that by separating from the addictive boyfriend she was faced with her own addiction to perversion.

She begins a session shortly before a holiday break with these words:

> Today I have the feeling again that I am hanging upside down and I could slide backwards ... You looked at me strangely when you greeted me, as if something wasn't right with me. I have the feeling my head is red hot but I haven't been doing anything strenuous ... [short break] I've just noticed that I'm kind of waiting, don't really know what to do with myself, but it isn't necessarily out of the ordinary.

Later in the session she talks of having had a 'tortuous' night, and that she feels she is living in a parallel world, 'as if I return to a dark world when I can't come here'.

I would suggest that when she is faced with loss she 'hangs upside down' – she returns to a dark world where she is excited /red hot – but if she is upside down her head is below – that is I believe that it is her genitals (below) that are red hot. And that she thinks the analyst looks at her in a strange way – perhaps he is excited too.

It later emerged that she herself is 'addicted' to obsessive thoughts about those Jews in concentration camps who had the role of dealing with the dead bodies after they had been gassed, and removing from these bodies, for example, the gold in their teeth.

And I think the painful depiction of the abuse is that she extracts the 'gold' – the excitement from this appalling scene, both the scenes in the concentration camps but also the experience, when she feels that the analyst is ('excitedly') looking at her upside down – at her lower parts. And so, I think the damage done in sexual abuse is not so much to the body of the child but to the mind. Jordi Sala speaks of the abused children feeling that they are 'bad'. One aspect of that may be the excitement (gold) that is extracted, or generated, by the abuse. Perhaps even she pretends she is dead to hide the shameful excitement. And this 'concentration camp' is the dark place she goes back to. Here she is both victim and is (secretly) extracting excitement. So that the 'gold' she can extract from the situation is that she can be the victim, and not have to take responsibility for her own triumphant excitement.

And the guilt would be compounded by the excitement of replacing mother with father – but then she feels both triumphant (red hot) and perpetrator, responsible for her mother's depression – this mother who constantly demands that she should make her mother better. And so, I think the patient feels 'bad' about her own excited sexual feelings, and about her triumph over the mother in being the one 'chosen' by her father. And she then feels responsible for her mother's depression. She feels that she needs to carry the burden of guilt. Yet this seems so unfair.

I think the dissociation which Jordi Sala stresses in these cases may become so entrenched because the guilt is so overwhelming – and at the same time there is such a grievance about the unfairness of having the burden of carrying so much guilt.

I also want to suggest that often the parents in these cases not only turn a blind eye but frequently, I think, the other parent plays a part, and takes secret vicarious satisfaction from the abuse – like a mother who sat knitting, being ostensibly constructive, whilst her husband, the father, beat their daughters; look, she seemed to be saying, my hands are clean. And I suspect that Sam's parents might now, too, become dissociated from their own guilt, by trying to 'shame' their son and their 'friend' (see Chapter 1). So that when Sam and the friend deny guilt, they may also be mimicking, or identifying with, the parents' denial of guilt.

To go back to the small boy, whom I quoted at the beginning, it seems to me that the particular burden that these abused children carry is unmanageable shame and guilt.

3 Child abuse as confusion of tongues

Luis Jorge Martin Cabré

In many of today's psychoanalytic theorisations, which build upon Ferenczi's contributions about the theoretical and clinical aspects of trauma theory, trauma is considered to be an invasion – of passion, love folly or hatred towards some other – into the subject's ego.

Ferenczi developed his theory of trauma starting from his clinical experience with borderline cases, and he presented it in his final works, especially in his famous work on *Confusion of tongues between the adults and the child* (1932), where he attributed a crucial role to external objects in the structuring of the child's psychic apparatus, and he underscored two essential arguments for psychoanalytic theory: identification processes and the splitting of the ego. By extending the seduction concept that had been theorised by Freud, Ferenczi made a considerable theoretical advance, as he presented the traumatic aetiology as the result of a 'psychic violation' of a child by an adult, a 'confusion of tongues' between them, and above all a 'disavowal' (*Verleugnung*) on the part of the adult over the child's despair.

Splitting and autotomy

When the adult's language of passion, which unconsciously manoeuvres the eroticism of both love and hate, clashes violently with the language of tenderness of the child, and the adult disowns and disavows any acknowledgement of those thoughts and affects in the psychic apparatus of the child, who had deposited all his/her trust in the adult, a trauma takes place that provokes not only fear, disappointment and pain but, above all else, inevitably leads to a splitting. In contrast with *Spaltung* (splitting) in Freud, according to which a part of the ego accepts reality while the other disavows it, in Ferenczi's conception a part dies and the other lives on, but devoid of affects, remaining excluded from its own existence as if it were someone else who was living its life. In addition to splitting, infantile trauma may generate fragmentation, atomisation and autotomy. We would underscore this last notion of autotomy, which in the biological sciences refers to the shedding of a body part, that is, the tail in reptiles, limbs in crabs, arms in octopuses. For Ferenczi, autotomy implies the amputation of a part of oneself, so from a Ferenczian perspective a part of the subject 'dies' through splitting. It does not feel pain because it does not exist anymore. Even more, '*he is no longer worried about breathing or about the preservation of his life in general. Moreover, he regards being destroyed or mutilated with interest, as if it is no longer his own self but another person who is undergoing these torments*' (Ferenczi, 1932, p. 6, italics added). The psyche defends itself by means of its self-destruction, or else by destroying whoever offers help or affect.

Therefore, the concept of trauma, and above all the idea of psychic commotion that would be described years later by Ferenczi in the *Clinical Diary* [1] refers to an unstoppable *breakdown* and to a loss of identity, with the consequent submission and unconditional docility produced by the traumatic experience, which destroy the ability of the ego to psychically elaborate it, as is the case in the fascinating clinical description he gives of his patient O. S. There we read about the loss of the sense of time, '*as though life did not have to come to an end in old age and death*' (Ferenczi, 1932, p. 142, italics added). But, as is the case with other living beings, this autotomy is not a defence mechanism, it is a survival mechanism. Paradoxically, the purpose of this extreme response arises to save one's life. To safeguard one's spirit and integrity it is necessary to sacrifice the living portion of the body and submit oneself to a self-treatment, to an autotomy in which the person has to abstract oneself both from oneself and from others. Would not this make us think of psychosis?

But in a previous work, *On the Revision of the Interpretation of Dreams* (1931), Ferenczi had already discovered that splits in the ego deriving from early traumatic experiences were defence mechanisms antecedent to the emergence of repression. As Ferenczi said, '*no memory traces of such impressions remain, even in the unconscious*' (Ferenczi, 1931, p. 240, italics added).

As a consequence, in his theoretical concept – later developed by him with greater precision – trauma becomes transformed into something that is not represented in the psyche. The reaction to pain belongs to the order of the irrepresentable and is inaccessible to memory and recall. From this point of view, for Ferenczi the trauma 'presents' itself, instead of being 're-presented': its presence does not belong to any present time, and it even destroys the present in which it seems to introduce itself. It is, then, a present without presence, a crazy present, in which the subject exits time while trying to place his or her unthinkable suffering into a greater temporal unit, outside of any everydayness or historical temporality. This is an infinite and inexhaustible present, but at the same time it is completely void.

Hence, Ferenczi places his theory of trauma in the dimension of a 'present' that remains outside of the historical temporality. Unlike the historical present, in which a presence and identity are settled, in this traumatic present everything is dissolved: there is neither subject nor opposition between subject and object. What Ferenczi suggests to us is that, in the dynamics and time of the trauma, something is hinted at that must do with death and cannot be represented. To Ferenczi, this is in fact '*a process of dissolution that moves toward total dissolution, that is to say, death* and the loss of a sense of time … *as though time were suddenly something infinite, as though life did not have to come to an end in old age and death*'

(Ferenczi, 1932, p. 142, italics added). But, perhaps, more than to a death that sets a limit, what Ferenczi refers to is to indefinitely dying, in a time in which nothing begins. Time is mummified and, acting as a death tissue, prevents and paralyses the function of the *après coup*. To Ferenczi, this is in fact a process of dissolution that moves toward total dissolution, that is to say, death.

But confronted with the impossibility of being represented, the body becomes the only addressee of the traumatic memory. That memory, bound to stay inside the body, enslaves the latter in the role of a spokesperson and transforms it into a martyr of the word that has lost its voice. The only chance of relief for this body lies in rebuilding the trauma and placing it back in the intersubjective space of the transference/countertransference of the psychoanalytic relationship. But, how? By means of what therapeutic instrument?

Subsequent developments

After Ferenczi's death, his 'scandalous' ideas about trauma, as well as the technical innovations derived from them, seemed to vanish from psychoanalytic theorisation. However, seemingly through a process of silent transmission, several of his most brilliant intuitions eventually managed to return, were reconsidered from quite divergent theoretical formulations, and they opened new paths in psychoanalysis.

While for Freud trauma as a consequence of a sexual seduction had been the key factor in the aetiology of neurosis, for Ferenczi it was the expression of a disorder in the communication between the child and the adult, a 'confusion of tongues'. This linguistic dimension would offer a point of contact with some of Lacan's conceptions, for whom trauma would be close to his concept of 'the real'; it would resist symbolisation and language, and consequently be unassimilable. If we configure the Oedipus complex as the ultimate expression of the symbolic order, the sexual incest that Ferenczi was referring to could only be understood as a breakdown of this order and as a 'confusion' among the registers of the Real, the Symbolic and the Imaginary, that is, among an unassimilable experience, truth and fantasy.

For Ferenczi, trauma is placed in the context of the relationship. Unlike the Freudian conception, where trauma determines the destiny of the drives, in Ferenczi, trauma modifies object relations, both with the external object and with their internal representations. Klein's (1935) conception of the good object as a container for the baby's projections seemingly is close to the tenets of her first analyst.[2] If for Klein trauma is defined in relation with the frustration of internal impulses and the projection of rage over bad objects and the subsequent defensive introjection, her followers, the so-called post-Kleinians, would not fail to underscore the important role of the frustrating real experiences as agents for the intensity of the child's destructive desires.

Ferenczi brought in the discussion about the innate nature of the drives. His thesis on the exogenesis of the neurosis became the first draft of a psychoanalytic psychology and of a theory of object relations. Outstanding authors in object relations theory, such as Fairbairn or Guntrip, adhere almost literally to Ferenczi's conceptions. This theory contributed to a progressive broadening of the concept of trauma. Traumatic situations arise from inadequate caring on the part of primary objects. Many analysts, Bowlby among them, attribute the disorders in the emotional development of the child to the inadequacy of early maternal care. Mahler's assertion that the real behaviour of the primary object bears a fundamental importance for infantile development has an analogous meaning.

Building upon Ferenczi's observations and incorporating some of Freud's ideas to the theory of object relations, Balint (1969) proposed a three-stage theory of trauma, emphasising again the effect of disavowal on its genesis. But perhaps the author who most faithfully recovered the intuitions of Ferenczi was Winnicott. Among his most significant theoretical contributions, we have his extension of the concept of trauma and his conception of *relative trauma* (1953) as a consequence of a 'not good-enough mother' regarding the functions required by the child. Following these observations, Khan (1963) coined the concept of 'cumulative trauma' highlighting the effects on the child of the fractures in the para-excitation function of the mother. This extended perspective on trauma would include also: the distinction introduced by Kris (1956) between 'shock trauma' and 'strain trauma',[3] Greenacre's (1952) thesis about 'screen memories' that conceal traumas, Waelder's (1967) idea of 'constructive traumas' in psychological development,[4] Sandler's (1967) 'retrospective trauma', Ekstein's (1963) conceptualisation of the difference between 'positive' and 'negative' trauma, as well as Baranger et al.'s (1987) distinction between 'pure trauma' and historicisation. Drawing on Winnicott, Green (1982, 1986) stresses the 'negative hallucination of the mother' and proposes the concept of the 'dead mother' as a screen for an irrepresentable void.

Ferenczi also theorised the fundamentals of a psychology of early disorders, and discovered previously unknown primitive defence mechanisms, especially splitting, the psychological consequences of which would be developed years later by Winnicott in his theorising of the concept of 'false self'. While Bion does not study the effects of trauma but rather psychotic thinking, he describes the splitting and fragmentation mechanisms that allude to self-destructive processes of the ego, or parts of it, and to their expulsion from the psychic apparatus. Several paragraphs of his works on the development of schizophrenic thinking (1956) and on the differentiation between the psychotic and non-psychotic parts of the personality (1957) are evocative of some of Ferenczi's descriptions in the *Clinical Diary*.

Challenges in contemporary clinical practice

If traumas of a sexual nature which prevent the development of the ability for enjoyment pave the way to sexual inhibitions, frigidity and above all phantasies and sadomasochistic pleasure, the traumas of a non-sexual nature destroy the sense of faith in the world and the transitional space that enables the feeling of being in harmony with others, of being the bearer of desires and of projecting oneself into life through an internal world dense with thinking and emotions. When a child feels that his thoughts and emotions have been systematically disavowed and neglected, his or her emotional and affective world is affected in its entirety. The child has now to reconcile his or her yearning for good-enough parents with the disavowed reality of not having found appreciation for his or her love. An apparently normal adolescent may become structured around a child who has been wounded and deprived of a shared emotional world, but behind the adolescent a person will be hidden who will not have a free and confident emotional field available, and one in whom the unelaborated traumatic experience destroys the possibility of perceiving him or herself as a whole person. And here we have the origin for a possibly perverse or psychotic structure, or dynamics.

We are still far from having reached an integration of all the parameters that remain open in psychoanalytic theory, starting with the challenge posed by the clinical experience with traumatised patients who develop attitudes, mechanisms and an organisation of emotions of a perverse, psychopathic or psychotic nature. However, when listening to patients who practise sadomasochistic relationships, or certain compulsive situations of physical self-harm through supposedly aesthetic surgical interventions, with issues of anorexia/bulimia, or with the unexplored issue of incest, either practised by fathers or mothers, problems of physical abuse and humiliation of women or children, the unwarranted cruelty towards persons who are in a weak or submissive position, torture in all its aberrant forms of application, racism and xenophobia, war, hatred and ultimately, perhaps, when confronted with a world that seemingly is not willing to renounce to a single drive, it leads us as psychoanalysts to wonder about what devastating experiences have been accumulated in that non-repressed unconscious to which I referred earlier, which are responsible for so much violence and destruction.

Perhaps reflection on the relationship between trauma and other pathologies may allow us to think that there will always be a need for the existence of psychoanalysis, which can offer itself as an alternative to quick or pharmacological treatments or therapies, because as Piera Aulagnier said, most of the time the patients do not come to our sessions looking for an intellectual answer or the deciphering of a truth; they come simply because they need to count on the help of a human presence, able to understand their pain, but above all able to enable them to go on being.

Notes

1 *Clinical Diary*, 26 June (1932, pp. 140–3).
2 Melanie Klein underwent an analysis of several years with Ferenczi. Once settled in Berlin, she undertook a second analysis with Abraham that would be dramatically interrupted by the unexpected death of the latter.
3 'Thus it seems that we are not always and only rarely with the desirable sharpness able to distinguish between the effects of two kinds of traumatic situations; between the effect of a single experience, when reality powerfully and often suddenly

impinges on the child's life – the shock trauma as I should like to call it – and the effect of long-lasting situations, which may cause traumatic effects by the accumulation of frustrating tensions –the strain trauma as I would like to say' (Kris, 1956, p. 54).
4 Building upon the ideas of Greenacre (1967) about the dangers of traumas in the pre-oedipal stage, Waelder highlights how the mechanism of transformation from passivity (stuporous reactions) into activity (shouting, reacting or escaping) is an index for a better resolution of the traumatic impact.

References

Balint, M. (1969). Trauma and object relationship. *International Journal of Psychoanalysis*, 50: 429–435.
Baranger, M., Baranger, W. & Mom, J. (1987). El trauma psíquico infantil, de nosotros a Freud. Trauma puro, retroactividad y reconstrucción. *Revista de Psicoanálisis*, 44 (4).
Bion, W. R. (1956). Development of schizophrenic thought. In *Second Thoughts*. London: Heinemann Medical Books, 1967.
Bion, W. R. (1957). Differentiation of the psychotic from the non-psychotic personalities. In *Second Thoughts*. London: Heinemann Medical Books, 1967.
Ekstein, R. (1963). Pleasure and reality, play and work, thought and action as variations of and on a theme. *Journal of Humanistic Psychology*, 3: 20–31.
Ferenczi, S. (1931). On the revision of the interpretation of dreams. In *Final Contributions to the Problems and Methods of Psycho-Analysis*, ed. M. Balint. London: Hogarth Press/New York: Basic Books, 1955. Reprinted: London, Karnac, 1980.
Ferenczi, S. (1932). *The Clinical Diary of Sándor Ferenczi*, ed. J. Dupont. Cambridge, MA: Harvard University Press, 1988 . French edition, Paris: Payot, 1985.
Green, A. (1982). *Narcissisme de vie, narcissisme de mort*. Paris: Minuit.
Green, A. (1986). Le travail du négatif. *Revue française de psychanalyse*, 50 (1): 489–493.
Greenacre, P. (Ed.) (1952). *Trauma, Growth and Personality*. New York: W. W. Norton & Co.
Greenacre, P. (1967). The influence of infantile trauma in genetic patterns. In *Psychic Trauma*, ed. S. Furst. New York: Basic Books, pp. 108–153.
Khan, M. M. R. (1963). The concept of cumulative trauma. In *The Privacy of the Self*. London: Hogarth, 1974, pp. 42–58.
Klein, M. (1935). A contribution to the psychogenesis of manic-depressive states. *International Journal of Psychoanalysis*, 16: 145–174.
Kris, E. (1956). The recovery of childhood memories in psychoanalysis. *Psychoanalytic Study of the Child, 11*: 54–88. Paper presented to the Midwinter Meeting of the American Psychoanalytic Association, New York, on 4 December 1955.
Sandler, J. (1967). Trauma, strain and development. In *Psychic Trauma*, ed. S. Furst. New York: Basic Books, pp. 154–174.
Waelder, R. (1967). Trauma and the variety of extraordinary challenges. In *Psychic Trauma*, ed. S. Furst. New York: Basic Books, pp. 221–234.
Winnicott, D. W. (1953). Psychoses and child care. *British Journal of Medical Psychology*, 26: 68–74. Based on a lecture given to the Psychiatry Section of the Royal Society of Medicine, March 1952.

4 Todd

The analysis of a latency-aged boy who self-harmed

Mali A. Mann

This analysis is of an 11-year-old boy who was referred to me by a colleague who saw him in therapy for a brief time. His analysis started shortly after he moved to California. Todd's presenting problem was his repressed anger with his underlying depression, skin picking and hair pulling.

His parents divorced when he was 9 and his father stayed in the city where the whole family used to live. It was his mother's idea to move to California after the divorce. The judge granted physical custody to the mother and visitation rights and joint legal custody to his father, which made it difficult for his father to travel frequently enough to spend time with his son. Todd's problems manifested fully when he was 5 years old. He had a history of self-harming and hair pulling from a very young age that coincided with his parent's marital discord. Todd's trichotillomania and self-harming behaviour escalated around the time his parents' divorce was finalising.

He is a very bright, articulate youngster whose mother lacked the capacity for emotional attunement. When she became frustrated with him, she hit and physically punished him. She was unaware of the importance of her parental responsibility and of developmental maturation as a parent. She was ill-prepared to be a parent and ambivalent about becoming one.

Despite parental resistance to analysis and significant maternal psychopathology, Todd's innate capacity to reflect, and his wondering about his own mind, his desire to make deep and empathic connection with people, especially maternal figures such as teachers and myself as his analyst, helped him to stay engaged effectively in his work with me. Additionally, his high intelligence along with his obsessive character structure made his analysis effective and successful.

Mother

The mother is a highly educated woman in her field who for several years had tried to become pregnant with her husband. They attempted IVF several times, but the mother was ambivalent about pregnancy and motherhood from the beginning. Her husband convinced her not to give up hope and to continue multiple use of IVF treatments. Finally, at 42, they were successful in becoming pregnant.

As a mother, she was inconsistent in giving care to her son. However, she moved Todd's nanny with her to California after the divorce. She often became quickly reactive and misread the emotional cues of her son. She delegated her mothering role to the live-in nanny, whom she hired when Todd was 6 months old. Todd's nanny was generally nurturing and maternal towards him. However, whenever a heated argument arose between Todd and his mother or when she lost her temper and struck him, his nanny would not interfere to protect Todd. She was afraid if she intervened, it might cost her her job.

From Todd's perception, the nanny was ineffectual in providing him adequate comfort and reassurance when he fought with his mother. Todd reported that 'she would put on a blank face' which made him feel confused. He expected his nanny would protect him out of a sense of loyalty and bonding to him. He wished she would stop his mother from hitting him and actively intervene.

Father

The father is an educated man in his own field, teaching physical education in a college, who has suffered from a long-standing depression for many years. He was warm, affectionate and nurturing, but he was described as being passive by his wife. Their marital trouble predated Todd's birth.

A stormy end to the marital relationship

The parents' marriage ended in a sea of turbulence, chaos and bitterness. When Todd started to see me everyone, especially Todd, was struggling to find an anchor of stability and a holding environment. He was 11 years old when he entered in analysis with me after a brief twice-weekly psychotherapy. I worked consistently with his mother, primarily in 'parent work'.

When his nanny was asked to leave (fired) by his mother because of financial trouble, he could no longer come to see me four times a week. His mother kept promising that she was going to rehire the nanny soon. It took about three months of waiting before he resumed his analysis again, identifying his intense anger and developing capacity to regulate himself when he was close to losing control.

I also actively worked hard with his mother to put a stop to her physical abuse. When she was confronted about her abusing behaviour, she became ashamed and kept repeating that physical punishment was part of her upbringing experience and it was culturally sanctioned where she grew up. She admitted that she frequently witnessed her father punishing her brother with his belt. She was spared because she was a good student and did not misbehave.

This period of my parent work with her was a challenging time, since I was unsure if I could bring the child abuse issue to the attention of the Child Protective Service. On the other hand, Todd was struggling about not wanting to know if he could feel his angry feelings towards his mother. He denied he was angry with her. Acknowledging his rage was a terrifying feeling and he feared he would lose control of his mind as did his mother. Eventually, during our work, he learned to get in touch with his feelings of anger and could own his angry feelings. He could use his anxiety about his anger as a signal to stop his self-destructive behaviour. He became quite good at it to the point that he could tell what would trigger his mother's angry reaction and pre-emptively read her feeling state to avoid having a conflict with her. He felt he was ahead of the game and could beat his mother in catching it fast enough not to become the target of her anger.

It was noticeable that he was on his way to consolidate his sense of self-worth, self-identity and self-independence. He wanted to be seen for his own autonomous self. He wished to be heard by his mother, to have his feeling state understood by her, and appreciated for being the person whom he was, for his own merits and flaws. He believed his mother never loved him, and thought possibly she wished he had never been born.

Todd hoped to become a star athlete in football and golf. His articulateness and intelligence were positive protective factors that helped him to feel assured that he was being heard by me, unlike his mother who could not hear him out. He felt that I understood him well and he expressed openly his wish to be my one and only patient.

Through the use of my interpretive work and the use of words that described and named his feelings, I was able to contain his anxiety steadily; I was able to help him to recognise and identify his feelings and become better in regulating his own affects. As I interpreted his conflicts consistently, the intensity of his anxiety gradually diminished.

Todd developed a solid working alliance with me. We were a good fit and he liked seeing me. I was like a wished-for mother in the transference. In the countertransference, my primary concern displayed itself in the form of my full-scale effort in the parent work I planned to do with his mother, especially the emphasis and specific focus I placed on her maternal neglect and abuse.

Todd had learned to isolate his own feelings whenever he noticed parental dispute and disharmony before the parents' divorce. Earlier in his life, he learned how to distract himself from his own feelings. He struggled with his earlier pre-oedipal needs and conflicts for a stable, predictable and genuine maternal figure. He was born into a world of ambivalence with a mother who had significant inner conflicts. The mother's attachment to Todd was ambivalent, insecure and showed the absence of emotional attunement. On one hand, she kept her marital affair secret for a long time, and did not want to tell Todd the truth and the real reason for their move to the West Coast. Todd heard it from his father, but wanted to hear it first-hand directly from his mother. She kept denying it despite his insistence on wanting to know the truth. On the other hand, Todd's nanny engaged in a robotic nanny duty, escorting Todd to his appointments without demonstrating any emotional expressiveness or caring.

Todd used to call his nanny 'my nanny'. As his analysis progressed and as he was more aware of his adolescent inner turmoil and his positive transference feelings, he came to call her by her first name. His nanny rarely waited for him in the waiting room, but more often waited in her car in the parking lot of the building.

I felt that I was the holding figure for his mother, the nanny, his father who talked to me on the phone regularly and all their narcissistic needs, as well as Todd's.

Todd's cats were important 'attachment' figures for him. Their symbolic presence representing his inner life was noteworthy. He was attuned to his cats' affective states. He noted their capacity for closeness and their sense of independence; he gleefully made jokes about the similarity of his cats' emotional state and his own feeling state of mind. He identified with them, especially with Molly. Once I interpreted that Molly replaced me when he was not in my office. He paused for a few minutes and smiled. My name as Mali and his cat's name as Molly rhymed and it sounded intriguing to him. He had not thought about it until that moment.

Todd was quite eager to see me and he was proud to discuss his wide range of interests – political, social, cultural, sports and literature – with me. He had a strong desire to share his interest in computer games with me.

Through his play, he could express his conflict over his anger and also his questions and doubts about his sexual identity. He wondered if he would end up getting attracted to boys and not girls. Specific identity questions and the themes of who he thought he was came to the surface frequently in his play material.

Todd read a lot and brought the articles he was reading, especially Stephen King's books, to his sessions. Then, he asked me if I had read them. It seemed his interest in types of books he read were both counterphobic and also a sign of his enactment. He wanted to see if I found these books disgusting as his mother did.

Todd expressed emerging sexual feelings towards girls when he spoke about his female classmates. He admired girls with good minds who excelled in their studies. I interpreted his desire to be admired by me as his wish for a perfect mother whom he could love and would be loved in return. His vulnerable self that wished to be loved by me came alive in the play room. It played out often through his questions about my patients who were leaving my office before his appointment time with me.

Todd's high intellectual ability and keen perceptiveness helped him to identify with his teachers, coaches and his father as his role models. He also used his charm and ability to deceive friends and his mother. This was an important theme that came up frequently, especially when his mother's secretiveness about her infidelity was not disclosed for an extended period of time. Todd knew from his father that his mother had had an extra-marital affair and refused to talk about it openly.

He felt identified with his father and perceived his mother as being a rejecting and abusive figure. He developed a theory that every girl he met was going to reject him. He talked in defence of his father and was very angry with the man who stole his mother from his dad and him. He said once 'he *robbed* me of my childhood happiness'. He felt demeaned by his mother, since he too felt betrayed. Consequently, his self-esteem became even more fragile. Todd on multiple occasions repeated in an angry tone of voice that he knew she had had an affair. He sounded like he was trying to convince me of his truth. He identified with his father's pain and sense of betrayal.

I encouraged his mother to have an open discussion about her secretiveness with Todd. He was relieved when she finally decided to discuss it with him, rather than denying it persistently as she had done in the past. This had a positive impact for both mother and son. He felt relieved that the secret was finally out in the open. The superego conflict began to transform to a less harsh and punitive one in the second year of his analysis. The revenge phantasies about the man who 'ruined his father's and his life' subsided gradually.

He was scared imagining how his angry feeling became unleashed and he would lose control of his mind. At the same time, the idea of a revenge and murder phantasy was ambivalently satisfying to him. Sometimes it made him feel scared because he knew he was just a lonely child, and was scared that nobody cared about him in this big wild world. He felt good that I was there for him to contain his 'worries', sense of insecurities and fears. He often pretended that he came to see me earlier than his appointment time in the waiting room, but told me he forgot to turn on the light signal. He took delight when I came into the room and took him to the consultation room.

I interpreted that when I found him in the waiting room, he felt that he needed to pretend by appearing indifferent to my acknowledgment of his presence. However, deep inside he was happy to see me, and he knew that I cared about him, even though he struggled with a feeling that I might have forgotten him between his sessions. He said, 'I just forgot to turn the light on!' I said, 'This is your way of making sure that I cared about you, and you feel you are loved by me.' He was quiet for a minute after what I said. After a brief pause, Todd said, 'Today, I wanted to know if you were coming out of your office and looking for me. I know it is silly of me to think this way. You know, my mom does not even know if I am in my room or not. I might as well sneak out of the room and go to the park. I did it once. She never noticed it.'

He told me that sometimes he felt guilty for pretending that he was sleeping in his bed, but he tried to stay out by climbing down his window and going to the nearby park on a few occasions in the very early hours of the morning. I told him that he wanted to make sure his mother cared about him enough to find out that he was in his room or not. Also, this was his way of wanting to know if I cared that he was there in my waiting room.

He felt badly when he talked about his 'manipulative behaviour' (as he labelled it), his lies and cheating. He felt it was better for him to be honest with me by letting me know about his negative side.

Once he developed stomach ache when he tried out for the football team. He realised 'it was his big worry feeling that went into his stomach' and he could not help himself. In his football team, he played the offence and he played to win. Todd had difficulty falling sleep at night, because of his multitude of worries. Likewise, the same problem of stomach ache and sleep difficulties happened when he invited a girl to his school winter formal. He got stomach ache each time he had a try-out for a sports team. He also worried that he would get kicked out of the gifted program even though it seemed highly unrealistic. This was an expression of his underlying insecurity and sense of dread that he would get disinvited from the program. His perfectionism was a defence against the fear of rejection and of being let down. His excessive focusing on detail was another aspect of his obsessive character that allowed him to ward off his feeling of insecurity.

After many months of playing out his violent phantasies in the form of drawings or playing board games, he could express his feelings of hatred toward his mother. He could verbalise his hurt, disappointment, hatred and anger toward her. I told him that he was afraid that if he had angry thoughts about his mother, it would hurt her for good, and he would feel hurt as well. He nodded and said 'I am happy for her that she now sees her own psychiatrist, she only sees her psychiatrist once a week. I see you four days a week!' He had a big smile on his face when he told me that.

Todd's exceptionally high intellect and analytical ability made him feel different from other kids. He reflected that his classmates did not think about social/political issues. In some ways, it made it more difficult for him to develop friends.

Presently he plays football, baseball, hockey and golf. He no longer worries about not having friends. He no longer wears a baseball cap to cover his baldness. He has a head full of hair. He made several close friends and does not feel inferior. Although it was easier for him to relate to adults he became aware of the importance of his peers' presence in his life. Todd is further along in his individuation process and has made progress toward developing an autonomous sense of self.

Earlier on, he denied having had any pain when he picked his skin, or pulled his eyelashes or hair. Somatic conversion and self-injurious behaviour were no longer present at this stage of his analysis.

Although he made significant analytic gains, Todd still continued to struggle with his ambivalent feelings towards his mother. He felt uncertainty about his future and worried that his impulsiveness still erupted and would make him lose control.

He told me that he has mafia blood from his father's side of the family. He also knew that divorce had occurred in his family for 'several generations'.

Todd has shown less rigidity at a conscious level to detect his own identifications with both of his parents. He came in frequently in his football outfits or with his golf clubs, showing me he identified closely with his father's sportsmanship. He is intent on wanting to get a football scholarship and go to the best university that is known for its prestigious team.

I wonder about the meaning of his hair pulling. It could be a displacement upward of genital masturbation as well as relief of inner tension. He might be ridding himself unconsciously of his unacceptable impulses. He reports that he no longer has a sense of shame for having had bald patches on his head, which made him a target for school bullies. It looked like an unconscious masochistic wish, perhaps like when he hit himself on the head. I also wondered if it might have been a castration issue. There is considerable evidence for the transgenerational transmission of castration fears. In reviewing his family background, it is reported that Todd's paternal grandmother cut his paternal grandfather's skin on the palm of his hand with a knife in a state of rage. Todd's father witnessed this violence as a young child. He was also afraid of his own angry outbursts which erupted like a volcano unexpectedly, and its destructive flow made Todd terrified.

I believe that the experience of tension relief was multi-determined; it perhaps goes back to the early mother–infant non-attunement state, when the infant's bodily care was not fused with adequate love, thus resulting in symptom formation. His eczema also could be viewed analytically as a form of expression of a lack of good enough maternal holding and containment.

Todd is able to identify his angry feelings more effectively, especially toward his mother. He allows himself to speak assertively to her and not avoid the subject at hand. Likewise, he can negotiate well about his analytic hours when he is scheduled to see me or when it presents conflicts with his sport commitments.

He is very interested in becoming a criminologist, which is in some way rather similar to my work with him as an analyst. On another level, he strongly identifies with his father's interest in sport, wanting to get perfect scores in his football, baseball and golf to make it to the best school through getting recruited for his superior athletic ability.

Countertransference

Todd and I were a good fit. I liked working with him. He saw me as a wished-for mother. My feeling about his mother's superego issues evoked a sense of wanting to help Todd even further. I have been concerned about his superego development. His mother lied to me on more than several occasions. Todd was aware of his mother's shortcomings and with his newly formed reflective capacity could anticipate his mother's feeling state.

When his nanny was fired, Todd was grief stricken. His mother did not seem to care about the continuity of his attachment figures.

My parent work and my analytic work with Todd taught me a great deal about the importance of the role my capacity played to contain the mother's anxiety, as well as Todd's. Meanwhile I believe the ego structure building, affect development/affect regulation and formation of capacity building for a mentalising process has been in full progress.

His mother's hatred of men in a symbolic castration issue seems to be intergenerational and there is evidence of how intergenerational transmission of castration anxiety can persist, should there not be a solid analytic intervention.

An extreme solution to his fear of destructive phallic aggression was manifested in his aggressive attacks during football games and competitiveness with other boys over the same girl he was sweet on.

My countertransference response included my submission to his seductive story-telling behaviour and my wish for him not to give up his phallic narcissistic and exhibitionistic strife. My wish to create a safe environment for him manifested by me keeping track of his interaction with his mother and helping him not to get intimidated by her or fall victim to her aggression.

The analysis continued to explore Todd's conflicts over his aggression and observing his compromise solution in the analytic process. His analysis has been complex, lively and rewarding.

Todd's process notes

Below are two sessions, one is an early session and the second is from a more recent analytic hour.

An early session

He came into the room without his baseball cap on his head, showing patches of baldness, and looking nervous or excited. He told me he is very angry with his mother who moved them here to California, far away from his father.

T: I lived in Florida for six or seven years (the state he had to move from) and I lived in Kansas City for two years before coming here. We moved to California with two of our cats, Oscar and Mollie, but our dog passed away before our move here! My nanny came with me too. [As he was relating the information about his recent move, he became angrier and made no eye contact while he looked visibly uneasy.]

A: *It must have been very hard to leave your father, your friends, your home and your therapist behind, and come to a whole new place.*

[His voice softened up and continued to tell me that his analyst's office was bigger than mine.]

T: I heard good things about you. [After a short pause, he said] I brought my cat, Oscar, for you to meet him. He is in the car with my nanny. You don't mind me bringing him here? I thought you might want to see him.

A: *Having Oscar accompanying you today makes you less worried whom you were going to see, especially when you have never met me or worked with me. You also want Oscar to meet me.*

T: Would you let me go and bring Oscar now?

[He got up quickly without checking with me to find out if I was going to give him permission to bring his cat inside the room, and he headed toward the door. After a few minutes, he entered the room with a big black cat, Oscar, in his arms.]

T: Oscar sleeps with me. Sometimes Mollie wants to sleep with me too.

A: You like it when Oscar and Mollie choose to be with you. It seems like it is very important to you that I should get all you tell me straight away and learn about everything about life at the start of our work together.

T: Yeah, this way we are off to a good start if you know all the facts.

[He kept the cat in his arms until he started to squirm. He took the cat to his nanny in the waiting room and returned to the session. He looked pleased with himself for showing him to me.]

A: It seems like it is important to you to want to make sure that you introduce everyone in your family to me, including your cats, and make sure that no one is left out.

T: [He made a grunting sound and nodded in agreement. He went on to say:] My nanny's dad got killed in action. He started with headache. He had a brain tumour. She went to live with her uncle. She started to work for a nanny agency and that is how she came to live with us.

[Then he told me how much he likes playing football, baseball, hockey and golf.

He said his father is a physical education teacher and likes talking about sport and watching it on TV.

As he was talking to me, he started pulling his hair. He pulled out one strand of his hair and showed me the root of the strand. He said] I want you to see the bulb at the end of my hair, I cannot help it. I do not know how it all happens.

A: You mean to tell me that the hair pulling you do is confusing to you? You tell me it happens without you intending to pull. It just happens without your control.

T: I do not feel any pain. Soon after I do, I see another bald spot on my head and lots of hair everywhere on my clothes. Not all my old classmates from Kansas gave me a strange look. Only a few would say nasty things to me. Believe me, I was not doing it to get their attention. I just could not help myself.

A: You wonder how I might be able to help you with your hair-pulling and your skin-picking problems. You want me to figure out what is going on in your mind. You also want me to understand your feelings of not knowing when you can't help yourself.

T: I have too many intense feelings that take over my head.

A: Pulling your hair is like trying to get rid of your bad feelings that are unbearable.

T: Yeah, sometimes I have voices in my head and I cannot get rid of them. My mom is making it worse for me. She pushes her ideas on me all the time. She is also a big liar. She thinks I am the one who lies. Lying runs in our family! My other therapist B could not help my hair-pulling problem. Have you seen anyone like me with so many bald patches? I don't mind wearing my baseball cap all year round!

A: There are lots of questions that we have to sort out as we get to know each other better. But for now, we must stop in a few minutes.

T: It looks like you have a sand box there in that corner! I want to play in the sand box when I see you tomorrow. You have got all those boxes there and I want to see what are inside. My nanny brings me here tomorrow.

[He looked serious when he said this in a serious tone of voice.]

A more recent session

At this point he continues his work with me, but there are some days that he misses his sessions because of his extra-curricular sports practice. Sometimes his football practice conflicts with the frequency of his four-times-a-week analysis. He developed the capacity to be reflective and is happy that he has a head full of hair. He dresses more fashionably, more like a preppy middle schooler.

On this session, he walks into my consultation room with a serious look on his face.

T: Just for you to know I got A plus in history, in science I got 68%, AVID 92. I need to get my math up. Science was F, it is all because I missed one week of work. I worked hard to get it up to C plus. English is my strong subject, but I got B there too. My mom is not happy with me because of that. See, I got my thesis done on one of William Stafford's poems. You must know his poetry and know who he is. He got the United States Poet Laureate. I like his poems.

A: *You want to make sure that I know him, and this way you assure yourself that I understand you and your feelings better when you talk about him. Your enthusiasm shows me that you like him through his poetry.*

T: Yeah, he is a pacifist though. I am going to work harder on my essay this time. I know I can get my grades up.

A: *You see your grades are not exactly at the level you want them to be. You want to show that you can do better work which will prove your superior ability.*

T: Yes, I *can* show I *can* do well too in the next quarter.

[After a pause, he said] My mom does not want me to go and see this movie, but I want to see *The Godfather*. She saw part of it with me, but she stopped it half way through. It is so frustrating that she does not explain why and just stops it. Did I tell you that she does not hit me anymore and she seems to be listening to me more?

A: *This must make a big difference for you, and you can perhaps relax around her better.*

T: I still get mad at her for not letting me see a movie. What's wrong to see the movie in the middle of the week? I think you would let me see it if you were my mom. Wouldn't you?

You understand why I like to see *The Godfather*. My father's families belonged to the mafia, and my Italian American background is my reason for wanting to see it. Mom does not understand how important it is to me. This is a special occasion. I am mad at her. She says the sky is blue and then says, 'Todd, you said the sky is yellow'. I think she has a memory problem. Is it really a memory problem or she can't help lying? She lied to my father!

She does not believe me. She accuses me of lying. I just repeat myself to make sure that she would hear me out. She thinks I changed my position, but in reality she is the one who says one thing and then claims that she had never said it.

A: *Now that you are leaving to spend three weeks with your father it makes it easier to tell me what you don't like about your mom.*

T: Yeah, Now I am hungry and tired. Do you have a granola bar or fig bar?
[I handed him the snack. He is hungry a majority of times when he comes to my office.]

She is going to be in Paris, she will spend her time with that man, her friend! I don't worry about her.

I love to live with my Dad. I wish I could stay with him and did not have to come back to live with her.

A: *Talking about your big intense feeling makes you hungry and tired especially when you are to leave for your holiday. You will not see me for three weeks. You do not talk about that.*

[I thought his request for food was his way of assuring himself of getting nurturance and warmth from me. This way he makes sure our connection is not ended, and that he can take something of me with him on his trip.]

T: I do not know, but I have been having a stomach ache the last two days.

I think you are right about not seeing you for three weeks has something to do with it. Maybe my stomach ache is telling me something about how I feel inside, just like now, I know pulling my hair out had to do with me getting rid of my bad feelings inside. See, for some reason this holiday, it feels longer than other times. I won't be seeing you for three weeks! Can I call you if I need to talk? I know you would say yes.

Conclusions

The trauma literature indicates that neglected children represent the largest segment of child protective services cases. The adverse impact of neglect may exceed that of impact of child physical abuse. My psychoanalytic case presentation represents how a child who is 'unwanted' by his mother and was subject to maternal deprivation and abuse develops a fantasy of not being loved by others.

In one of the studies of mother–child relationship disturbances, motherhood could be seen as an unfolding developmental plan activated by the birth of the child. The mothers in the study fell into the category of those whom Anna Freud called 'unwilling mothers' (A. Freud, 1955).

The psychological effect of Todd's neglect and abuse triggered a threat to his physical integrity of selfhood and compromised his sense of self-value and self-esteem. The psychological unavailability of his mother resulted in attachment problems.

There is no such thing, to paraphrase Winnicott (1960), as an abused child, no such child, that is, separate from the world of his actual relationships. Todd was exposed to his mother's abusive experience and he was an unwanted child. In Todd's case, we can see how he had reacted to his psychologically unavailable mother who delegated the task of motherhood completely to the nanny and was unresponsive to the child's signals, especially the child's pleas for comfort and understanding.

His psychoanalytic treatment facilitated his emotional development through the use of interpretation and the analyst's presence as a developmental object.

He could bring his affective needs into the therapeutic relationship, feeling safe and 'feeling held'. He also was able to develop a capacity for better self-regulation as he felt more stable internally. Fortunately, his mother's plea for help was a favourable sign in providing Todd with a structured psychoanalytic containment and developmental object that offered him the formation of new internalisation. Anna Alvarez (2012) describes stages in the process of recovery from abuse and how there needs to be faith in a non-abusing object. That seems to have happened during Todd's analytic treatment.

References

Alvarez, A. (2012). *The Thinking Heart*. London: Routledge.

Freud, A. (1955). *Safeguarding the Emotional Health of Our Children: An Inquiry into the Concept of Social Work: Case Work Papers*. New York: Family Service Association of America.

Winnicott, D. W. (1960). The theory of the parent–infant relationship. *International Journal of Psychoanalysis*, 41: 585–595.

5 The abused child – a sad, never-ending story
Some observations on abused children in the current refugee crisis

Marianne Leuzinger-Bohleber

Personal preliminary remarks

I first planned to summarise some of the clinical findings with abused children in our ongoing psychoanalytic prevention projects. But sometimes times change dramatically: as the director in charge of the Sigmund-Freud-Institute (SFI) in Frankfurt, I am – since October 2015 – intensively engaged in a special service for traumatised refugees in the frame of our outdoor service at the SFI. I am also responsible for the pilot project STEP-BY-STEP trying to support refugees in the arrival camp Michaelisdorf in Darmstadt. I would therefore like to share some experiences, clinical observations as well as some psychoanalytic conceptual considerations. I will focus the question if and how we, as psychoanalysts, may contribute to the attempt to help some of the severely traumatised refugee children and adolescents in the acute societal situation. As psychoanalysts, we have a broad knowledge how destructive man-made disasters might be for the traumatised and their offspring. Can we contribute to decrease the probability that the traumas will determine, often in a hidden destructive way, not only the lives of the adult refugees, but also those of their children and even grandchildren?

Introduction

The so-called refugee crisis surprised politicians, citizens as well as other such professional groups including medical doctors, social scientists and psychoanalysts. 1,091,894 asylum seekers were registered in the EDV system EASY (Erstverteilung der Asylbegehrenden) in Germany in 2015. Daily media reports confront us with the enormous suffering and despair of the refugees and their children. In Germany, these reports may evoke memories of the 14 million refugees in the aftermath of the Second World War, particularly among elderly people. The individual and collective memory of human catastrophes connected with war, terror and flight might be one of the reasons for the surprising wave of warm welcome, as well as the willingness of thousands of Germans to offer their support for the refugees on the one hand, while on the other hand, an alarming surge in violence and hostility towards refugees may be observed. Each day refugee homes are subjected to arson attacks!

After the Paris, Brussels and now Würzburg and Munich attacks, concern among the German population has increased with respect to Islamic terrorism and radicalisation. This is due to the fact that several hundred thousand refugees have not been vetted in Germany. German experts have expressed their alarm as Salafistic preachers seek to radicalise adolescent refugees, above all, in the arrival camps for refugees (see Wikipedia: Flüchtlingskrise in Deutschland, 2015).

Thus, ongoing intensive discussions are underway focusing on a possible split within German society. One reason for the ambivalent and diverse reactions to refugees may be that war refugees also evoke unconscious associations with the term 'trauma';[1] in other words, extreme experiences that expose the self to fear of death, helplessness and powerlessness, thereby inundating it in such a way that fundamental confidence in a helpful object and an active self collapses.

The biologically rooted flight impulse is among the ubiquitous reactions to the perception of trauma and traumatised persons. It is the impulse to look away, to deny and to turn a blind eye to the unbearable. In order to be able to turn empathically towards traumatised refugees and immigrants, invariably an emotional strain, it is necessary to counteract this impulse. This has proven particularly difficult since the current situation reminds people that severe trauma in the context of so-called man-made disasters not only burden or even destroy the lives of one generation, but are often transmitted to children and grandchildren.

Can psychoanalysts contribute to this current urgent and complex societal situation? Over the foregoing weeks, we have been confronted with this question daily, particularly in the context of an exclusively psychoanalytic research institution, the SFI (see www.sigmund-freud-institut.de). I can only briefly mention two of our engagements: a) working with refugees in our outpatient service and b) supporting refugees in an arrival camp (STEP-BY-STEP project).

Working with traumatised refugees in the framework of a psychoanalytic outdoor service at the Sigmund Freud Institute: one example

The different psychoanalytic institutions within the SFI, Centre for Psychoanalysis in Frankfurt, offer specific crisis interventions and psychoanalytical therapies to refugees. We have built up a professional network which discusses specific challenges and treatment techniques with this group of patients. Colleagues from the organisation FATRA (Psychosoziale Beratungsstelle für Flüchtlinge und Folteropfer (Counselling Center for Refugees and Victims of Torture)) have offered several training courses on specific questions of treatment (for example, work with translators and so on) communicating their experiences with traumatised refugees since the Balkan War in the 1990s.

In this context, I will summarise the first experience of crisis intervention with one adolescent refugee: 'I don't want my sister to follow me from Eritrea to Germany' (Mr. A., 17-year-old refugee from Eritrea). Mr. A. was referred to me by his social worker following drastic weight loss and suffering from a dangerous psychosomatic state. He has no will to rise in the morning and has stopped attending school.

I was shocked when first seeing this young man: he seemed to be bordering an anorectic state, had a 'frozen' facial expression and appeared to be severely depressed. He attempted to communicate with me in English and in German, which proved difficult. He told me that he had not talked with his parents for several weeks. I suggested that he try calling them from my phone at the institute. Sadly, he reported that his 14-year-old sister had left his parents two weeks ago and they had no information as to her whereabouts.

He agreed to have a second talk with a translator. In this second interview, he talked about his traumatic flight. He left Eritrea since he would have otherwise been drafted into the army for years. His parents did not want to take this risk. His father had also been in the military for years and had experienced terrible things. He is now handicapped. The family is very poor. He flew to Sudan where he was captured by criminals who wanted to extort money from his family. They captured him and held him prisoner for four months in a forest. He almost died from hunger. He was tortured several times. His thigh was severely mutilated by a burning nail to prevent him from fleeing. Only once the criminals understood that his parents were unable to provide the ransom did they let him go. He went through other severe traumatisation during his flight through the Sahara and the terrible weeks in Libya where he was tortured and nearly died. He was finally able to flee and to secure a place in a boat to Lampedusa. Some of the people on the boat drowned. He eventually succeeded in reaching Germany a year previously. He smiled for the first time in the interview when he talked about the operation in a German clinic which helped him to heal the deep wound in his thigh: 'I even can play football again – Germany is good!'

At the end of the interview he talked about the fear for his young sister, that she may be exposed to 'similar terrible experiences as I had been. She's probably in the same place in Sudan in which I was. I think about her constantly, particularly during the night.' He breaks down when talking about Libya. He witnessed the brutal rapes of young women there.

I interpreted:

> I understand that you suffer severe depression because you cannot protect your young sister, and feel responsible for her as her older brother … This is very hard to bear. But you are not responsible for the terrible situation in Rwanda and Libya. Of course, you would like to help your sister, if you could … You probably think you have to give up all the positive things in your current life – your good achievements at school, your health and your good perspectives for your future here in Germany, because you feel so guilty.

This interpretation obviously reached him. The social worker reported that he started to eat again and to go to school.

He is presently unwilling to accept more therapeutic help but prefers the connection to the Eritrean community in Frankfurt. The Eritrean translator had opened doors to the large and well-established subculture in Frankfurt. As this example may show, often the psychoanalytic understanding of inner reactions to trauma (as in this case a kind of survivor guilt) proves to be fruitful in working with refugees in crisis interventions, particularly if the refugees are still in adolescence (see Leuzinger-Bohleber et al., 2018).

STEP-BY-STEP, a pilot project supporting refugees in an arrival camp in Darmstadt

Particularly due to the psychoanalytic knowledge on trauma and its transgenerational transmission, the SFI, in close cooperation with the Anna Freud Institute, has been engaged in early prevention in several projects within the institutional framework of the Excellency Initiative IDeA since 2003 (see, for example, Leuzinger-Bohleber & Lebiger-Vogel, 2016; Wolff, 2014).[2] Based on empirical studies on around 3000 of traumatised families with a migrant background (predominantly refugees), in October 2015 the Ministry of Social Affairs of the State of Hessen requested that the SFI conceptualise the pilot project STEP-BY-STEP in an effort to support refugee families in a 'first arrival camp' in Darmstadt. As a model project, it will be scientifically evaluated in order – should it prove successful – to then be implemented in other first arrival camps in Hessen. Here I can only shortly describe some of our first experiences since the project's start in January 2016.

Those politically responsible seek to accommodate particularly vulnerable groups of refugees (mothers with infants travelling alone, families, pregnant women and in particular traumatised refugees) allocated to Hessen, in Darmstadt itself. In keeping with the above-mentioned SFI psychoanalytic prevention projects, STEP-BY-STEP provides initial professional support by way of close collaboration with local teams. In the long term, support will be intensified with the help of additional steps in view of the fact that the families in question are supposed to be allocated permanent housing in Darmstadt or its environs. This makes it possible for STEP-BY-STEP to offer further and even long-term support for the integration of these traumatised refugees within Germany (see for example, Leuzinger-Bohleber & Lebiger-Vogel, 2016).

On what concepts is the psychoanalytic project STEP-BY-STEP based?

When arriving in the Michaelis Village the SFI, together with a group of colleagues and students from the Goethe University, offer several daily modules – in close cooperation with local teams – which seek to create minimal secure orientation for refugees; first holding and containing experiences in reliable, empathetic and professional relationships. An indicator of this attempt is, for example, that the institution is not called 'first arrival *camp*', but instead 'Michaelisdorf', a metaphor for a social meeting place, a welcome in a social community where everyone should be an idiosyncratic individual and personality, with their specific (trauma) history, their vulnerabilities, but also their specific gifts, talents and capabilities. These individual capabilities, professional skills, etc. should be recognised, supported and taken up in specific, productive forms contributing to the social life within the village, even if the refugees should only stay in the village for a few weeks.

The village thus first tries to offer refugees security and protection. The feeling of uprooting, loneliness and insecurity are actively counteracted trying to prevent a reactivation of the traumatic experiences of helplessness, impotence, extreme despair, pain and panic resulting for example in nightmares, flash backs and so on. Consequently, everyday structures, contacts, but also the relationships among themselves are crucial: it is supposed that an initial feeling of community, of an initial arriving and belonging – as in village life – will arise because, as many studies have shown, this is not only important for a sense of 'welcome' in the host country but also because it strengthens the later willingness of the foreigners to integrate. To strengthen social cooperation, the project's goal is that each resident (of any age) receives about two hours of each day to be actively supported ('to receive something'). Furthermore, each resident should offer her or his own activity for two hours each day by personally carrying out one activity for the village ('to give something').

STEP-BY STEP consists of the following psychoanalytically based modules.

Supervision of the supporting staff at Michaelisdorf

Specific work with traumatised refugees, as well as the continually changing institutional situation, presents a huge challenge to the local social support team, as well as the medical team. Weekly psychoanalytic supervision for the whole team has proved extremely helpful, both for understanding the psychodynamics of individual traumatised refugees and their families and as typical countertransference reactions for coping with traumatised individuals (see for example, Bohleber & Leuzinger-Bohleber, 2016). The psychoanalytic supervision also helps to meet the danger of being overfilled and overtaxed, to maintain professional borders, and to thus prevent burn-out, depression and psychosomatic reactions among 'helpers'. It also proved helpful for enhancing the professional flow of information.

To give one example: in one supervision, the team reported that a single mother, Mrs A. from Afghanistan, had withdrawn to the confines of her room for five months and had been 'forgotten' by the social support team because of the chaotic situation during the first weeks in the Michaelisdorf. One day the mother asked the medical team to take away two of her four children 'because I feel overtaxed'. In the supervision, we discussed the guilt feelings of the social workers and the necessity of not splitting off such 'failures', but to reflect on them professionally in the supervision.

After the session, I visited the woman together with a translator. The woman is in a dangerous psychic state. She hallucinates and has paranoid fantasies: she says that the father of the four children had hired a criminal gang to take the children away from her and to take them back to Afghanistan. The four children are obviously also in a bad psychic state: all of them were lying in bed (at 11 a.m.), and seemed severely depressed and apathetic. During the talk with the woman, the 'Medea fantasy' (Leuzinger-Bohleber, 2001) came to mind. I feared that this mother could do harm to her children, one likely reason why she wanted to 'give away' the two younger ones in a kind of emergency action.

We immediately organised a daily support for Mrs. A. We organised several crisis intervention sessions. She declined medication but seems relieved that she receives daily psychological support. The children are brought to the daily kindergarten and language courses. We were also able to arrange for the family to be transferred to secure accommodation in Darmstadt where she will be cared for by a social worker. STEP-BY-STEP has organised psychiatric assessment for the woman and further steps for the whole family (such as kindergartens, school, individual partnership or long-term therapy for Mrs A.).

In subsequent supervisions, we discussed the full range of observations and interventions. We organised a regular, systematic check of all the families in the village by the social support team to prevent some of the (depressed) refugees from once again being 'forgotten'.

Weekly psychoanalytic assessments and crisis interventions for traumatised refugees in cooperation with the medical care service and the social work team

Each week experienced psychoanalysts offer psychoanalytic assessments and crisis intervention in acute situations with traumatised families, children and adolescents (see example above).

Psychoanalytically oriented FIRST STEPS groups for pregnant women and women with babies/infants

Two-hour, weekly group provisions for pregnant women and mothers with infants where current topics on early parenthood under migration circumstances are discussed and mother–child interactions professionally promoted in a culture-sensitive manner.[3] Some women from the group of refugees are motivated to participate in the groups as 'co-group leader' (co-adviser) ('to give something').

Many young mothers developed severe postpartum depression due to the traumatic experiences in their home country as well as during the flight. Many of them had been victims of violence and rape. Some of them asked for termination of a pregnancy which had been the product of violent rape. Due to the professional network of STEP-BY-STEP we could provide such (late) interruptions of pregnancy in a proper clinic and offer some psychoanalytic crises intervention before and after the termination.

All these women came to the FIRST STEPS groups afterwards and were supported in their mourning process as well as in their motherhood with their other children. Most of the refugee mothers are very young and have many children. Often the mothers speak the same language and are beginning to establish contact with each other, a crucial step for integration.

Psychoanalytic (painting) group for children

Psychoanalytic child psychotherapists visit the daily kindergartens and language classes for an early recognition of children in need of special support. These children are sent to weekly child therapeutic (painting) groups held by an experienced child and adolescent psychoanalyst. In these groups children are given the opportunity to express their burdensome experiences, or even traumatic experiences, and are thus able to communicate their experiences to the professionally trained therapist. Many studies have shown that it is very important for the processing of traumatic experiences that children are not left alone with their experiences, but rather, are encouraged to talk about them in a protected space within a psychoanalytic setting. Some women from the group of female refugees are asked to support the painting groups, for example, by translating ('giving something').

One 6-year-old boy repeatedly depicted his experience in Syria where he had witnessed a suicide bomber in the shopping area of his city. The father told the therapist how disturbed his son had been afterwards. He started to stutter, had severe nightmares and aggressive outbursts.

A first crisis intervention can take place in the therapeutic group in the Michaelisdorf. The boy as well as the family will need long-term psychoanalytic help once they have found sustaining accommodation in Darmstadt.

Psychoanalytically oriented groups for adolescent girls and boys

Psychoanalytically oriented groups focus on the interests of adolescents. Further provisions for particularly distressed adolescents will be provided, as the case may be, in addition to students of the Goethe University Frankfurt and a staff member of the SFI. Some fathers and mothers from the village have also been asked to become involved in the provisions ('to give something').

In the first sessions of a group for male adolescents, SFI staff members painted the rooms of the Michaelisdorf together with the adolescents to create a meeting place for the latter. Some adolescents painted the Syrian flag on the wall of the room. This resulted in the decision by Afghan adolescents to cease attending the group. Then, with the help of translators interesting and challenging discussions were initiated among the adolescents: a joint meeting place in Germany must provide space for refugees from different countries, from Syria as well as from Afghanistan and other, for example, African countries. These talks initiated first reflections on adolescent topics, such as identity, religion, culture and democracy.

Language courses for different age groups

Daily language courses for pre-schoolers, elementary schoolchildren and adolescents as well as adults are offered.

(Educational) evening programmes for adults

SFI staff members and professional therapists, together with staff members from the Michaelisdorf, offer evening programmes on various topics (for example, problems of the legal contemporary situation of the refugees and asylum seekers in Germany, value systems in democratic systems, but also nutrition-related aspects, sleeping problems, parenting style, German educational system, female roles and so on). Different resources can be used, such as movies and photo materials; the objective is to build trust through training programmes to – in the best case – avoid constellations of national groups within the Michaelisdorf and to facilitate conversations on difficult issues such as violence and/or prostitution.

It is a well-known fact that violence had erupted among diverse groups of refugees in the first reception camps in Germany (for example, violence between different religious Muslim groups). Thanks, perhaps, to the range of provisions afforded by STEP-BY-STEP, such violence has until now fortunately not been observed in the Michaelisdorf.

Conclusion

I have tried to communicate our experiences which indicate that psychoanalysis, due to the breadth of its knowledge for example on trauma and its transgenerational transmission, on early and lifelong development, parenthood, migration and flight may indeed add professional expertise in the support of (traumatised) refugees in a first reception camp, as well as in crisis intervention in psychoanalytic outdoor services.

I understand all these endeavours represent a mere drop in the ocean with respect to the besetting and complex social situation within the current refugee crisis. Nevertheless, it does constitute an attempt, in keeping with 'outreach psychoanalysis', to provide our specific expertise for the support of refugees.[4]

Notes

1 We use a narrow definition of trauma according to Bohleber (2010): The traumatic experience can be characterised as an experience of a 'too much'. The self is overfloated with unbearable pain, despair, helplessness often in combination with fear of death with long-term consequences. The basic trust in a helping other breaks down as well as a basic sense of an active self. 'Psychoanalytic trauma theories have evolved on the basis of two models, the one psycho-economic, and the other hermeneutic and based on object relations theory. To grasp the phenomenology and

long-term consequences of trauma, we need both models. The psycho-economic model focuses on excessive arousal and on anxiety that cannot be contained by the psyche and that breaks through the shield against stimuli. The model is based on object relations and the breakdown of internal communication which produces an experience of total abandonment, precluding the integration of trauma by narrative means' (Bohleber, 2010, p. xxi).
2 The IDeA Centre is an interdisciplinary research centre that studies 'children at risk' from different perspectives. Currently, more than 100 researchers from many different disciplines (such as educational sciences, neurosciences, psychoanalysis and developmental psychology) are cooperating. The centre is supported by the Excellency Initiative of the State of Hessen (see, for example, Leuzinger-Bohleber, 2015).
3 The project FIRST STEPS is a project for immigrant families, implemented by the SFI in cooperation with the Anna Freud Institute. The pilot study started in 2007. The primary study was implemented in Frankfurt in 2010, and since 2012 additionally in Berlin. The project focuses on the earliest integration of children with an immigrant background, supporting their parents in the critical phase of migration and early parenthood. By using a prospective randomised comparison group design, the effectiveness of a psychoanalytically oriented early prevention program (intervention A) is compared to the outcomes of groups provided for by paraprofessionals (intervention B). Intervention A is a professional provision supporting the immigrant families as based on developmental knowledge of early parenting, and combines home- and centre-based intervention. Intervention B is a centre-based provision by paraprofessionals with an immigrant background. More than 1000 families have been contacted in Frankfurt and Berlin. Here, 330 families decided to participate in the project and have been randomly assigned to intervention A or B. Around 140 have continuously taken part in the study in Frankfurt where recruitment has already been completed. In Berlin recruitment is still ongoing. The families are supported and assessed during the first three years of the children's lives until entering kindergarten. Social and family stressors, the quality of parent–child interaction, child attachment security, the affective, cognitive and social development of the children, and the children's physiological stress level during kindergarten entrance as well as the social integration of the families are assessed.
4 The first preliminary results show that professionally supported, good early parenting (Intervention A) improved the social-emotional, cognitive and language development of immigrant children as well as the social integration of their families. Due to the successful implementation of the project in Frankfurt, a further roll-out across Germany has started, and in addition to the implementation in Berlin another implementation of FIRST STEPS in Stuttgart is currently being undertaken (see Emde & Leuzinger-Bohleber, 2014; Leuzinger-Bohleber & Lebiger-Vogel, 2016; Leuzinger-Bohleber et al, 2011, 2012; Rickmeyer et al., 2016).

References

Bohleber, W. (2010/2018). *Destructiveness, intersubjectivity and trauma: The identity crisis of modern psychoanalysis*. Routledge.

Bohleber, W. & Leuzinger-Bohleber, M. (2016). The Special Problem of Interpretation in the Treatment of Traumatized Patients. In: *Psychoanalytic Inquiry* 36: 60–76.

Emde, R.N. & Leuzinger-Bohleber, M. (eds) (2014). *Early parenting and prevention of disorder: Psychoanalytic research at interdisciplinary frontiers*. London: Karnac.

Leuzinger-Bohleber, M. (2001). 'The Medea fantasy'. An unconscious determinant of psychogenic sterility. *The International Journal of Psychoanalysis* 82: 323–345.

Leuzinger-Bohleber, M. (2015). *Finding the Body in the Mind – Embodied Memories, Trauma,* and Depression. International Psychoanalytical Association. London: Karnac.
Leuzinger-Bohleber, M., Rickmeyer, C., Tahiri, M., Hettich, N. (2016). Special Communication. What can psychoanalysis contribute to the current refugee crisis? Preliminary reports from STEP-BY-STEP: A psychoanalytic pilot project for supporting refugees in a "first reception camp" and crisis interventions with traumatized refugees. *International Journal of Psychoanalysis.*
Leuzinger-Bohleber, M. & Lebiger-Vogel, J. (Hg.) (2016). *Migration, frühe Elternschaft und die Weitergabe von Traumatisierungen: Das Integrationsprojekt "ERSTE SCHRITTE".* Stuttgart: Klett-Cotta.
Leuzinger-Bohleber, M., Bahrke, U., Hau, S., Arnold, S., Fischmann, T. (eds). (2017). *Flucht, Migration und Trauma: die Folgen für die nächste Generation* (Vol. 22). Vandenhoeck & Ruprecht.
Leuzinger-Bohleber, M., Parens, H. (Eds.) (2018). Trauma, Flight and Migration. Special Issue of *International Journal of Applied Psychoanalytic Studies.*
Parens, H., Leuzinger-Bohleber, M., Brisch, K.H. (2018). Prevention in mental health. In. Akhtar, S. & Twemlow, S. (eds) *Textbook of Applied Psychoanalysis*, New York: Routledge, 267–287.

6 The making of an abuser

John Woods

Introduction

How is it that a child becomes an abuser? We know that abusers have generally been abused in some way when they were children (Finkelhor, 1983; Beckett, 1999), though not necessarily sexually (Bentovim & Williams, 1998). But only some abused children go on to abuse, just as only some go on to develop self-destructive behaviours. Clearly there are individual differences in the way children deal with experiences of abuse, differences perhaps in the way they have processed their trauma.

Psychological as well as physical trauma has been established by many studies as crucial in understanding the effects of child sexual abuse (Bentovim, 1996; de Zulueta, 1993; Herman, 1992). But what we mean by trauma is something that by its nature stretches the use of language because of its essential quality for the individual who is threatened with being overwhelmed with states of mind that may include pain, fear, anxiety, 'feelings that are too much to bear' (Horne, 1999, p. 268). They may also be too much to articulate by any means other than repetition. Evidently some go on to inflict that trauma on others.

Engaging therapeutically with the residues of trauma from the beginning of treatment has been essential in working with young people who have abused (Hodges et al., 1994, p. 305). Since not all children who have been traumatised by neglect and/or violence repeat those patterns, there must have been something different for these children in their response to trauma. Maybe it is only possible in retrospect to identify the internal processes affecting the development of a potential to become the abuser. Perhaps from psychotherapy we can infer the effects of earlier experiences on later development, even though it may be much more difficult to predict such consequences.

There is no such thing, to paraphrase Winnicott (1960), as an abused child, no such child, that is, separate from the world of his actual relationships. The child is a product not just of his specifically traumatic experiences but of a milieu in which power and control is exerted by someone (usually male), who has succeeded in neutralising a carer (usually female), to bring about the exploitation of a child (usually, but not always, female). The entirety of this interlocking set of roles has been conceptualised by Bentovim as a 'Trauma

Organised system' (Bentovim, 1996). I have proposed how this complex power structure has typically been internalised by the young abuser, and reproduced in action, not kept internal as it might be in the case of self-destructive psychopathology (Woods, 2003). He has identified with the aggressor as a form of protecting the ego from unacceptable feelings (A. Freud, 1936, p. 109–21), neutralised his own capacity to feel care or concern and stifled the vulnerable child within himself. Treatment can be aimed at differentiating and realigning these disordered identifications, but because the enactment of an abusive scenario has taken place in the child's external world, so a therapeutic intervention has to engage as much with the child's external reality as with his inner world. The case presented here demonstrates the interaction between these different facets of the child's experience, which can then be directed toward change.

A clinical narrative

It was with great relief that I said goodbye to my young patient in the waiting area. I was trying to maintain some semblance of good order but I was being ignored, pointedly. His foster mother paused, looking regretfully at him and me. I said, 'It's alright'. However, he looked at me coldly, said nothing, and they left. Back in the therapy room with a heavy heart I tidied up the broken toys and bits of paper strewn around and then, feeling a bit better, sat down and reflected upon another session ended early by me. I was not seeing my supervisor until next week. My heart sank at the thought of another two sessions to endure before getting her support. But her words, 'He is not there to make you feel good about yourself!' came back reprovingly. I looked at the gouge marks on the desk and wondered about this aborted session. Was he trying to tell me something I should hear, rather than be forced to stop? There was his message in front of me: 'FUCK OFF!' Well why shouldn't he tell me that? After all, what was I offering him? A cure for his unhappiness? Hardly. Could I, or anyone make up for his fractured life as a refugee? To stop him being hated and rejected by other children, and becoming unbearable to his foster mother, because of his behaviour? No, I was not going to turn him into a happy well-adjusted child. Or change his fate, to be reviled and excluded by society on account of his grossly sexualised aggression? Least of all could I correct the past sexual abuse against him by his original father. I thought of how my work with him had begun, and his initial presentation as an anxious, traumatised child, burdened with shame and anxiety; I had thought he could accept help by means of someone offering an understanding of his pain. Within a few sessions, however, any contact with me was rejected and now I was seeing more and more this look of cold hostility. When some conflict occurred and he felt he had to accept a limit, or climb down, sometimes literally, it was as though I did not know that child.

Rick, aged 9, was referred because of compulsive sexual behaviour, aggression, anal masturbation, encopresis, smearing, sexually molesting younger children, school refusal and false allegations of sexual assault against older children.

He was also described as showing signs of hyperarousal and going into states of dissociation. He had been removed from his original family, who were already traumatised refugees from a war-torn country. It was assumed he had been the victim of sexual abuse by his father from an early age, though he had always refused to confirm this. The disclosure of his father's sexual offending, and the mother's complicity, was from other children. The provision of a single foster parent from the same country of origin was not thought ideal by the social care department, but it was the best available option. Social workers specialising in helping refugee families felt at a loss with this case. The foster mother was fast approaching the limits of her tolerance. After an initial assessment, Rick was offered intensive psychotherapy, that is, three times per week concurrently with parent guidance for his mother, all of which eventually lasted three years.

I thought back to our very first session; he found a crocodile puppet and roared at me, as much with pain as with rage. Thus, I could see the child referred for attacking other children, sometimes in a calculated way but often in a fury, accusing them of assaulting him sexually when blatantly it was the other way round. I said that I knew he had been hurt and perhaps also frightened; therefore, he would want to frighten and hurt others. When there was no response to this I wondered more casually whether this was a creature that belonged in his country of origin. He dropped the toy monster immediately and began to explore the other puppets, asking me their names and identity. But as he dropped each in turn he seemed more hopeless. Attempts to discuss his thoughts or feelings about his country of origin, or having moved here, brought no response. In subsequent sessions, he went on to roll around the floor provocatively showing his bottom and laughing teasingly saying, 'you want me don't you?' Responding to this behaviour was not easy; my instinct was to react educationally, as it were, by telling him to stop such inappropriate behaviour, or by ignoring it. Later I learned that the behaviour was even more unacceptable in his original culture than here. However, the aggression conveyed was inescapable, and I was helped by my supervisor to convey that he was testing me to see if I wanted to do something sexual to him and needed to know that I would not. The behaviour changed, not that he seemed reassured, but rather resentful, as though I had pushed the abuse back into him. Thus, when he looked so coldly hateful, I began to fear the power he could exert by making an allegation against me in some form.

An article had just appeared in the *Journal of Child Psychotherapy* by a psychotherapist who was the target of a false allegation by a child in care. Despite a complete lack of any corroborating evidence he was suspended from work and investigated thoroughly, and traumatically (Ironside, 1985). The return of Rick safely to his foster mother was reassuring to me at least as much as it seemed to be for him, the nagging fear of my vulnerability made me discuss this risk with colleagues but despite their sympathy and understanding I realised there was little anyone could do. They might have absolute confidence in me as a person and a therapist, but if it came to an official investigation who could guarantee what went on behind the closed door of the therapy room? I began to realise the actual power of this child and the potential to in effect destroy me, not symbolically, but in reality; I was 'playing with dynamite' (Welldon, 2011).

The mess in the room in the early days of therapy had made me think that he needed to see whether I could tolerate his messy angry self. However, any brief calm that occurred, and any feeling of being together in the session led to sudden aggression and a heightening of anxiety. The only symbolic play he allowed himself was the crocodile roaring at me again. If he stopped attacking me he would subside into misery saying, 'I am just shit, I should not be alive'. He proclaimed that he would kill me, and then himself. It seemed that he could not stand the intimacy of the session and so I was careful to keep my distance, and yet he would refuse to leave the room at the end of sessions. His emotional confusion seemed alleviated by the cold look of hatred, as a sense of mastery was restored. Enlisting his foster mother's support at the end of the sessions enabled him to leave, but he seemed to feel outmanoeuvred, still cheated. Gouging the desk became a way for him to defeat any sense I might have of progress. After trying all the interpretations I could think of I finally had to warn him the session would have to stop. (I had established at the outset of therapy the rule 'No harm to anyone or anything'.) He challenged me bitterly: 'You try and stop me!' I got up and stepped away. He ran from the room and disappeared down the corridor. Since I was no longer in the habit of chasing after him, I went to the waiting area, whereupon he arrived with a look of triumph, but was at least calm.

The axiom of forensic psychotherapy is to find the *victim within the abuser* (Cordess & Cox, 1996). Parsons points out how violence can be a natural response to a perceived threat to the psychological self, 'in the absence of a protective other' (Parsons, 2009, p. 362). Clinical experience bears out the validity of finding traumatic roots of violence (de Zulueta, 1993), but there are multiple levels of complication since the victim self can also serve to hide the abuser. Alvarez (2012) shows how apparently 'motiveless malignity' is mobilised in order to protect the abuser from any feeling that he is in fact the victim. The abuser self can thus proclaim itself the victim. Sexualisation plays an important part in this process because of its power to both preserve attachment to a perverse object and protect against fears of abandonment (Glasser, 1996).

Rick's initial sessions showed him in touch with a victim self that could not be nurtured or healed. Shame at his dirty and despised self, however, then appeared to drive him toward violence. Suicidal thoughts and gestures came easily, as a form of revenge for the harm he had felt done to him. We can only imagine the traumatic social situation that was in the background of his life, but with his mind overcast, as it were, by the abuse from his father, Rick found it unbearable simply to be. The treatment relationship became a vehicle for this destructive dynamic. Any closeness to the therapist was felt as immensely threatening to him and had to be resisted by battles for control, and by sexualisation. This was a clear example of 'core complex anxiety', as described by Glasser (1996) in his analysis of the roots of sexual perversion. Rick was bringing his experience of being a victim of sexual abuse by his father, non-verbally; it seemed he was re-experiencing something of the abuse in the arena of therapy. The therapist would be standing in at times for the abusive father, but could instantaneously change to being identified as the child to be abused. The gestures of sexual submission were invitations for me to sexually abuse him, but in a way that would instead be his victory, and reverse the roles entirely. Thus, he could fulfil these contradictory roles; now as victim to me, but also then to become the abuser, making me the helpless victim. We were in a particularly vicious circle; he would continually test limits, forcing me to set boundaries, which made him feel abused by me; I was then made anxious that, accused of being the abuser, I would in effect become the abused child. In this way, I think I was made to feel the sort of existential terror that he must have felt at the time of abuse and that he carried with him as its legacy. Even the revulsion I felt at his sexual overtures must have been a replication of his own experiences.

Work with my supervisor enabled me to see this situation for what it was; out of a need to repeat the impact of being terrorised and helpless when abused, he was employing a massive projection of the abused self. I was forced to accept that there was no appeal to a more reasonable part of the personality, or to a coherent co-operative ally in this work; instead the abused self had come to find satisfaction in abuse, and traumatised as it is, it only wants to abuse further. I admit I wondered at times if after all that had happened to him in his short life, that becoming an abuser was the only possibility for him. On the other hand, if he could allow himself to be found by me back in the safety of the waiting room, and other moments like these, then perhaps there was a glimmer of hope.

Alvarez (2012) has pursued links with work on adult psychopaths, referring especially to the work of Meloy (1985). At times when I realised this child was using hatred to combat loss and vulnerability, I felt I was, in her words, 'looking evil straight in the eye'. In adulthood, a dependency develops into an addictive process where cruelty becomes desired as a substitute for the original lost object (Alvarez, 2012, 158). Fortunately for Rick, however, at the very least his immaturity as a child implied a possibility for change. I enlisted the help of Rick's foster parent.

Sessions with the mother present enabled me to regain a therapeutic role and to respond with comments addressing the need for us all to remain safe and not torment each other. Joint sessions proceeded for a time without interrupting her parenting sessions. Skilled parent work is of course essential in any child's psychotherapy but this kind of case requires an extra dimension. Workers with the parents and/or carers need to have a special resilience or flexibility in order not to be thrown by threats of traumatic re-enactments. I am indebted to my colleague Marianne Parsons whose sterling work with Rick's foster mother enabled the treatment, and us, to survive. The mother was able to overcome the crippling feelings of helplessness that Rick had induced in her, and as a third person she regulated the emotional contact between my young patient and me. Rick was calmer and had less need to provoke me or test limits. Perhaps there had been an original mother for Rick who was not totally taken over by the abuser, an early experience of something better that could be refound by him and located in the therapeutic space provided by his now pair of therapists.

With this safe structure to the sessions, a degree of symbolisation was made possible in his communication. And through play we could see more of the sadistic interactions that persisted in Rick's mind.

The King was a bullying father figure, forcing Punch to clean the toilets, but it was never done well enough, and he was screamed at, 'Do it again!' and would be made to go and live in the toilet. But Punch had a rescuer, the Queen, and together they plotted to defeat the King. There was much rehearsing and reworking of violent scenarios with the King beating, imprisoning and torturing Punch, followed by the Queen visiting him; she comforts and feeds Punch and gets him out of the toilet/prison in order to murder the King. It was not hard to translate these characters into an oedipal family drama, naming them generically father, mother and boy.

Further convolutions of the victim/abuser dynamic can be traced in this play. We can see how Rick's oedipal development was distorted by abuse. His father was no straightforward oedipal figure but had impacted in a very different way on the boy's sexual development. Rick seemed to envisage himself as castrated, annihilated, reduced to a faecal state of being that existed only to take revenge. He had lost both the caring pre-oedipal mother and was nowhere near an oedipal phase of development. He seems to have been left with no identity except to enact a projection of the abusive father, but while also identifying himself in a submissive pseudo-feminine form. Thus, he could maintain some kind of equilibrium by abjectly controlling any of his objects, a complete paradox of both abuser and victim. The only way for him to salvage some form of masculinity in the external world would be via an identification with the perverse father abusing other children. This would become a compulsion as he developed because only that way would he be able to fend off feelings of annihilation and despair.

Interpretations were made during these sessions by the technique of displacement (Melandri, 2012). My comments at this point were intended to reinforce the emotionally meaningful aspects of the drama, for instance the rage and fear in Punch, and sometimes his despair when he languished in prison. Links with Rick's own experience was not explicit. There was a triumphant pleasure at revenge against the King/father when he was made to suffer gross punishments for his wrongdoing. Parallels between these events and Rick's own life did not need to be spelled out. The stories I believe had their own power and momentum. Sadistic interactions, leading to healing resolutions, were now portrayed in the medium of play rather than enacted in the transference, and gave their own satisfaction to Rick's mind. Parental concern and the pain of empathy were represented by the figure of the Queen, and although Rick's mother was in the role of audience to this play, she also became involved and could sense I believed its symbolic importance. Other children appeared in the play, and as Punch was no longer being beaten and abused, stories of adventure and exploration became possible. Soon there were reports of changes for Rick at home, where there was less conflict and misery, and then improvements at school. The violence and abuse now taking place in play were still part of Rick's internal world, but available through symbolisation rather than being re-enacted. Interpretations were made not to reinforce his fears of abusiveness but to reflect his need for safety and wish to be understood. I would refer, for example, to the King, or 'father, who needs to be helped to stop being such a bully', *not* 'this bullying part of you that needs help'. The aim of this kind of comment would be to reinforce what seemed an appropriate defence, or sublimation, in play, not undermine it by reducing it to its original traumatic elements. Finally, Rick was able to share thoughts and memories, not all of them traumatic, about his country of origin. And he was able to talk about his wishes for peace in the country he still regarded as his.

Alvarez (2012) describes stages in the process of recovery from abuse and how there needs to be some faith in a non-abusing world, a sense of a non-abusing object. This would then enable both the remembering and forgetting. The remembering we can see here could now take place through a degree of symbolisation and the forgetting through an eventual rejection and disposal of the therapist some years later. But that as they say is another story.

Elsewhere I have proposed a treatment model adapted to the special needs of a child who has abused as well as been abused (Woods, 2003). Psychoanalytic psychotherapy is often held to be poor at dealing with acting out or anti-social behaviour (Roth and Fonagy, 1996), but with certain modifications it can be the treatment of choice for these patients, because of its adaptability to individual needs. The non-directive stance of the therapist is important since what the child brings to treatment cannot be predicted; neither can the therapist's responses be pre-determined by a structured treatment programme. Adaptations of the setting according to the child's needs, as in the case here, often need to be considered. There are, however, some general considerations for this kind of work; firstly, extra attention is required for the family system, or network of carers. The therapy needs to be seen as part of monitoring and keeping safe. Rick was fortunate in the positive relationship maintained by the foster mother, who could use the support offered her, but very often in the cases of youngsters who have abused, the family has broken down so that the child is left with a professional network that attempts to substitute for family. This is often fragmented and needs much work if the treatment is to be made viable. Secondly, anyone attempting to offer therapeutic work must expect repetition of the abuser/victim dynamic. These are traumata which do not fade, but demand expression. The victim in the child will seek out an abuser in the therapist, just as the abuser in the child will seek to create a victim in the therapist. Often these two threads will be intricately and dangerously wound together.

Do children who abuse constitute a distinct patient group? Maybe they do have characteristics in common, but as Judith Trowell (2007) observed in her detailed study of the effects of abuse on children at different stages, sexual abuse is not a diagnosis. A child who has sustained sexual assault adapts in a variety of ways, depending on circumstances and their particular characteristics. Psychoanalytic psychotherapy is a unique research tool that reveals the way in which traumatic responses can be deflected away from the self onto others, a process which leads to the formation of a young abuser. As the evidence of the individual story emerges, it also permits that narrative of abuse to be symbolised, restructured and possibly changed.

Finally, to come back to the original question: how did this abused child become an abuser? There can be no simple answer, but the course of the psychotherapy may provide at least some inferences; the relationship created by the child with his therapist bore significant traces of emotional trauma and victim/abuser dynamics. It is hard to imagine that a child unaffected by sexual abuse would have brought such issues into the treatment. The initial fear, appeasement and attempts at seduction of the therapist was but one layer of the child's responses to trauma; soon the tables were turned and the therapist became the one to be victimised, and controlled by hate. That twist of the transference derived from the imprint of the child's experience with the abuser, his perverse adaptation; that is, his ability to turn victimhood into the identity of an abuser. Fortunately, the parameters of the treatment enabled sufficient flexibility to provide an extra layer of containment in the setting, which was gradually internalised by the child.

Acknowledgement

Thanks to the Social Care agency and patient who gave permissions for the material, suitable disguised, to be presented. Thanks also to Mrs Marianne Parsons for her sterling help with the treatment and the paper, Mrs Zaphiriou Woods for her helpful comments on the emotional impact of the work, and to Mrs Anne Alvarez for her warmth, intelligence and generosity of spirit.

References

Alvarez, A. (2012). *The Thinking Heart*. London: Routledge.
Beckett, R. (1999). Evaluation of Adolescent Sexual Offenders. In M. Erooga & H. Masson (eds), *Children and Young People who Sexually Abuse*. London: Routledge.
Bentovim, A. (1996). *Trauma Organised Systems*. London: Karnac.
Bentovim, A. & Williams, B. (1998). Children and Adolescent Victims who Become Perpetrators. *Advances in Psychiatric Treatment* 4: 101–107.
Cordess, C. & Cox, M. (1996). *Forensic Psychotherapy*. London: Jessica Kingsley.
De Zulueta, F. (1993). *From Pain to Violence*. London: Routledge.
Finkelhor, D. (1983). *Child Sexual Abuse*. New York: Basic Books.
Freud, A. (1936). *The Ego and the Mechanisms of Defence*. London: Hogarth, 1968.
Glasser, M. (1996). Aggression and Sadism in the Perversions. In I. Rosen (ed.), *Sexual Deviation*, 3rd edition. Oxford: Oxford University Press.
Herman, J. L. (1992). *Trauma and Recovery*. New York: Basic Books.
Hodges, J., Lanyado, M. & Andreou, C. (1994). Sexuality and Violence. *Journal of Child Psychotherapy*, 20: 283–305.
Horne, A. (1999). Sexual Abuse and Abusing in Childhood. In A. Horne & M. Lanyado (eds), *The Handbook of Child Psychotherapy*. London: Routledge.

Ironside, L. (1985). Beyond the Boundaries. *Journal of Child Psychotherapy*, 21: 183–206.
Melandri, F. (2012). A Long Journey from Catastrophe to Safety. In N. T. Malberg & J. Raphael–Leff (eds), *The Anna Freud Tradition*. London: Karnac Books.
Meloy, J. R. (1985). *The Psychopathic Mind*. London: Aronson.
Parsons, M. (2009). The Roots of Violence: Theory and Implications for Technique with Children and Adolescents. In M. Lanyardo & A. Horne (eds), *The Handbook of Child and Adolescent Psychotherapy*, revised edition. London: Routledge.
Roth, A. & Fonagy, P. (1996). *What Works for Whom*. New York: Guilford Press.
Trowell, J. (2007). The Effects of Child Sexual Abuse. In C. Thorpe & J. Trowell (eds), *Re-rooted Lives*. London: Jordan Publishing.
Welldon, E. (2011). *Playing with Dynamite*. London: Karnac Books.
Winnicott, D. W. (1960). The Theory of the Parent–Infant Relationship. *International Journal of Psychoanalysis* 41: 585–595.
Woods, J. (2003). *Boys who Have Abused: Psychoanalytic Psychotherapy with Young Victim/Perpetrators of Sexual Abuse*. London: Jessica Kingsley.

7 The lost child

Laura Tognoli Pasquali

The happy consequence of a sexual intercourse between adults is, at times, the birth of a child. The tragic consequence of a sexual intercourse between an adult and a child is always the death of a child. This simple brutal truth is the heavy weight that hits the analyst when he becomes close to an abused child, or to someone who had been abused as a child.

It is not easy to come close to the area of solitude and pain of someone who has been abused because, as Luis Cabré wrote in his chapter, the earlier the trauma, the more incomprehensible and confused the experience of it.

Left alone, the child has no words nor images to express it and is unable to elaborate it. He is invaded by an unnamed anguish, by a deep discomfort, by an evil that becomes tarnished with guilt. It is best to hide this thing that hurts and is confusing.

Adults too, not just children, struggle to visualise an abusive situation, especially if the perpetrator is someone close, someone 'above suspicion', so it happens frequently that when the child finds the strength and the words to ask for help, he meets up with a barrier of disbelief and accusation that leaves him in the most desperate solitude.

To negate the evidence is easier than facing an unacceptable reality, so everyone prefers to forget.

Despite my hesitation, I have decided to share with you a very disturbing clinical situation.

Giorgio

Giorgio has been in analysis for about a year when we run into a very difficult analytic time. The sessions are slow, filled with facts and deprived of emotion. My interventions are flat, boring and pedantic. I feel that there is no life in them. What is missing are the magical moments that analysis brings by lighting the present with a memory of the past, or by making us feel the pleasure of touching something real, or giving shape to a desire, reawakening an interest.

Despite this, Giorgio seems happy to come to analysis, he is anguished when forced to miss a session and when he arrives he greets me with a big smile that instead of cheering me up, makes me feel guilty.

My feeling is that I am going around constricted orbits, pushed by a gravitational force unconsciously dictated by my patient or even by myself, a force that keeps me distant from him. We are both alone, unable to get in touch. As time inevitably progresses, I feel like drowning in a world with no insight.

Then one day I asked him whether he remembered a dream and he said: 'No, after the nightmare I talked to you about when we first met, I don't think I dreamt anything worth dreaming anymore.'

A dreadful dream comes to the surface of my memory: his grandfather, with a bulldog face, rings the doorbell. Giorgio is paralysed with fear. I know the nightmare goes on with an even more disturbing sequence but as much as I try, I cannot remember it: it is as though the second part of the nightmare has fallen into a black hole. Giorgio helps me to remember and the images reconnect with precision and shock inside me. The scene has changed, the time and the place are different. Giorgio and his girlfriend are trying to insert an anal catheter into their puppy to help it defecate but instead, by mistake, they sew up its anus. In the dream as well as with me, Giorgio is not particularly worried.

He was struck by our first meeting and remembers quite well what I said to him then. I told him that he was bringing me the image of a grandfather who was still there, beside him, like a bulldog who will not let its prey go. He rings the bell of the beginning of our analysis to show that he is even here by our side, more alive than ever and still able to provoke in Giorgio the same fear as long before.

I had told Giorgio that it was a great relief for him to think that he was not alone, he had now a partner to share the caring of his puppy, of something tender and little inside himself now invaded by smelly, bad things.

I had told him that he was depicting the analysis to get rid of all the rubbish and dirt he had kept inside: a sort of catheter fit for the purpose. We had also spoken of a different desire which was to shut everything down, forever, inside himself, and thus feeling cured and forever freed from a very damaging, hard experience. We both felt that the puppy with the sewn anus represented very well this tragic possibility.

While Giorgio spoke with extreme lucidity about our first meeting, I too was taken back to that first encounter recalling the anguish and distress evoked in me by the story that this handsome young man was telling. When he was very young, perhaps 3, his grandfather came into his room for the first time and since then, every Sunday, Giorgio felt compelled by promises, threats and blackmail to hide there with him. So, while mother cooked lunch, dad read the newspaper and the older sister was engaged with friends, the 'poor' grandfather, so alone after grandmother's death, was busy 'taking care' of the little child. The sexual requests became more intrusive and insistent, as time went on, and the threats more violent to ensure Giorgio's guilt-ridden and anguished silence. The abuse continued until the grandfather's death when Giorgio was 12 years old.

He told me his story with great sadness and much embarrassment and with some stealthy tears wiped away by a tissue rapidly hidden in his jeans pocket.

But suddenly he gathered himself together and with a big smile, assured me he had not thought about the abuse anymore and everything was now all right: 'that bad period has disappeared, there is no trace of it in me', he stated with some pride, 'even the difficulties with my parents have been solved'.

It is true that they had not believed him when, after his grandfather's death, he had picked up the courage to tell his big sister first and then his parents about the abuse.

It is true he had felt even more lonely and desperate when they had accused him of being a liar and making up the whole story. He was used to telling lies but this time he felt he had lost all respect from his parents and all his faith in them.

It is true that sometimes the anguish became unbearable and that he could not free himself of a constant sense of guilt, that he was afraid of being with a woman, that to attend an exam was like a nightmare … but now everything was fine: 'I have worked a lot on my anger and I feel cured. I am happy now, full of life, full of women, I want to look forward to life and I want to find a good partner.'

When I told him I felt that he seemed quite lonely carrying the weight of all the hidden tears in his pocket, his eyes filled up again and he allowed himself to let go, in a cry that had been kept inside for too long. It was then that he told me in tears of the bulldog dream. A dream that for a year I had abandoned in a corner of my mind, away from my awareness.

Right now, it is me who feels confused and guilty. If I think of the dream, it seems to me that now I can look at it from another angle and read it in a slightly different but substantially diverse way from how I had seen it when I had first listened to it.

Giorgio had confronted me then and confronts me now with two images suspended in time, images both contemporary and belonging to different ages of life. In the first, there is a child terrified by his monster grandfather, a child alone with him, an appointed victim of his mortal grip. In the other, there are two adults that do not allow a puppy to use his inside for the long, complicated process to feed and grow, eat and digest, absorb and defecate, clean and become dirty again, play and face reality.

Two adults concentrated in killing a puppy child, without realising it, with absolute indifference.

Since our first meeting, Giorgio anticipated what help I would have given him. I would have helped him to close the abuse for ever inside himself not allowing anger, pain or shame to still hurt him. I would have become an attentive companion in assisting him to bury into the alive flesh of his puppy, our analytical child, this dirty story of an abuse, a story no one wants to hear, a story that soils everything it touches, a story that can be only forgotten … and he nearly managed that.

It was a disquieting experience to become conscious of having unconsciously acted as a parent who helps the other to hide inside their little child bits of such smelly experiences that they can only come out of an anus as they cannot become words in the mouth. I would have never thought I would contribute to stop the growth of a child by forbidding him to talk of a haunting experience, of something so dirty as to become unbearable. A tough blow to my identity as an analyst!

Despite something having broken down in my certainties, dragging with itself a sad sensation of confusion and inability, I am also able to recognise that my enactment marked a turning point in the analysis.

My very insecurity made me more attentive and closer to Giorgio who in turn allowed me to enter areas of closer intimacy with him. I could even be admitted to see his tenderness and fragility: feelings he had strongly negated before and could now find a place in the analytical scene only after I had confronted myself with my narcissistic wounds.

When I had understood, on my own skin, how the pressing need to forget things fast creates a crystallisation of traumatic memories in a timeless present, the previously empty sessions became full of meaning that I could not see before. I saw how abuse with the constellation of emotions it carries within: anger, fear, triumph, excitement, indifference, anguish … and among all a devastating confusion is a constant master of the victim's dreams, fears and hopes.

We find the abuse there amongst us in the sessions, we feel it in the weight of the body, in the discomfort of words, in the sudden anxiety for a thought that has no reason to be there. In the mistrust, accusation, bewilderment. In the anger for a violence we can barely grasp when something is thrown inside us, even if it does not belong to us. In the sessions, we experience how difficult it is to maintain our own thinking, how the abused enters our mind with a sequence of submission and violent intrusion without leaving the analyst any time to reflect. Anger and solitude but also a great excitement pressing to go ahead and get pleasure from something physically dangerous that provokes shame and a great confusion that blurs everything up and makes it impossible to defend oneself. We feel how our thoughts enter the mind of someone who has been abused as if they were violating him or her again. We can touch inside them a blister of anger, bile and blood that mixed together to become paranoia, depression or masochistic dreams: the magma of madness.

An abuse finds infinite representations to express itself. The betrayal of a partner becomes an obscure evil that nests in the body and invades the mind. An examination turns into the fear of an invasion leaving behind a nameless anguish. Not being recognised subtly links itself to desperate devaluation: it is in fact very common for the abuser to gather all the pleasure whilst throwing on his devalued victim all the guilt and pain. Living these emotions again and experiencing them in the transference recreates the fertile ground that helps the buds to grow, withered branches to bloom and children to play again.

'It's as if we were playing frozen wolf', commented a patient once, 'do you remember when you had to freeze when caught by the black wolf, till a friend came and touched and you could run again?'

That game was not part of my broad repertoire of games as a child but I made it my own immediately hoping, despite my tender age, to have the possibility to play it again many times preferring, of course, the role of the one who frees her friend with her warm touch!

Often, however, I have been assigned the role of the frozen child or that of the black wolf that enters you leaving inside a deadening cold. It is not easy to tolerate it but when emotions get moving they create in the transference a dynamic situation where the characters may experiment being the victims and the aggressors and where beside a frozen child there is also someone who can touch him or her and give back the strength to move again: this is when the sterile and cold sessions animate with life which is anger, pain and fear, but also hope.

The most difficult analytic task is in my opinion to touch the paedophile, the seducer of children. Yet he too needs to be unfrozen. He too is stuck in a situation of abuse crystallised in an eternal present. We must wait by the perpetrators too although we know it is much easier to say, 'He hurt me a lot' than 'I contributed to shutting him up or sewing his anus'. We can see this both on a personal level and with our abused patients, with whom it is much easier being close to the pain and anger for what they have endured than touching that area of seduction and cruelty where it is difficult to understand who is the seducer and who is the victim.

It is even more difficult when a person we fear to be or we know as being a paedophile steps into our room and lies on our couch.

As well as the difficulty in managing our countertransference and the natural tendency to run away from what is disturbing and scary, I have the impression that to deal with perversions, the analyst is forced to explore a particular type of object relation that I believe has been neglected in analytic literature: I am thinking of Bion's theory of negative links (1967). The interchanging of envy and gratitude does not help us understand the behaviour of someone who is perverted. This alternation of passionate bonds creates a relationship of constant tension in which love and hate rule over each other alternatively, while the need for knowledge, though idealising or devaluing the object, will finally submit to reality and allow the instinct of life to rule over the instinct of death.

Perversions need another kind of ground to grow and develop. They do not blossom in the humus of passionate relationships but in the ground of no links. The mechanism which I think I have seen in action is not based on envy but on theft and is therefore not followed by gratitude, it is followed by concealing.

When you steal something, you are not grateful to your victim, you must hide the haul accurately, keeping it secret and showing it to no one.

The pervert will receive immense pleasure by only showing his pickings to whoever will allow to be tricked into believing it belongs to the thief, and then fall into the thief's net to become the victim of the stealing.

Seduction and negation are the weapons of the game, not devaluation and aggression.

It is a very difficult task to analyse perversions as you find yourself becoming a victim of the pervert precisely when you feel most sympathetic and close to them. This is where the presence of a third can be very useful, at times even indispensable to help in seeing these mechanisms in motion during analysis.

A child seducer takes us to a place where it is very easy to lose one's balance and sway unconsciously supporting their defences or becoming their accuser and in so doing leaving them at the mercy of their own perversion.

Marco

A young analyst came to me asking for help regarding a paedophile situation. Marco, a man disguised as an 'eternal adolescent', had asked for an analysis as he was afraid of his attraction towards 'real adolescents' with whom he used to surround himself and even more afraid for a sexual desire towards intelligent children who were able to talk like adults.

Marco fears his sexual needs that he feels as dangerous but at the same time can speak of them as his loving desires to help children grow, a legitimate love that only perverted minds could see as sinful. Marco's ambivalence was echoing into the countertransference of the analyst who felt seduced by the paedophile: somebody no one wants to listen to, and yet so needy to talk to her of his desires and even of some 'little acting out' that could become more dangerous if kept secret.

At the same time the analyst has the impression of being enmeshed by Marco and treated like an ingenuous girl who believes in the fairy tale of 'I help children grow'. She knows her patient needs help but she also feels seduced to believe him, and yet a moment after gets afraid that Marco wants to come to analysis only to find a witness to his good will.

Neither of them, Marco nor the analyst, can really wait by the paedophile: as soon as he gets touched he is immediately pushed away by both because they are frightened of him.

I think that in such a state of twilight the enlightenment can come from the trivial things that the intimacy of a session can bring to light through the experience of transference and countertransference, experience that feeds the need and the pleasure of understanding things together which, to my mind, is the beating heart of analysis, the emotion that give us the strength of facing the most disturbing aspects we find in our patients and in ourselves.

Therefore, I would like to try and revisit with you a session I chose amongst many as I think it shines a light on what I am trying to describe. A week of holidays has gone by since Marco had brought to analysis the unpleasant discovery of his sexual attraction – or maybe just fondness? – for a 10-year-old child, the son of a friend he had dinner with. The analyst had found this to be a precious opportunity to talk and Marco had seemed to her unhappy to have to leave analysis right when he was discovering it was the child's intelligence and his ability to 'talk like an adult' that made him so attractive to Marco's eyes and body.

After the week of holidays a smiling Marco enters the room and as usual goes through what he calls 'the removing', which is placing on the desk anything he carries with him: coins, keys, phone, tissues. He does it with slow and controlled gestures, then he goes to the couch. He slips on the way but quickly readjusts his balance and smiles again, asking the analyst if she has had a good holiday, then begins talking: 'I wrote to Filippo to thank him for suggesting to me to do an analysis, good advice even though I should have come here earlier. Anyhow, I really think that when I left you last week I put everything under the rug.' The session before the holidays had given the analyst great hopes and this latest statement greatly disappoints her. To recover that moment of grace, she reminds Marco how he had then felt relieved to be able to talk.

'Yes,' Marco answered, 'and moreover I could see that there is a problem, I even whimpered a little which annoys me a lot as it makes me feel stupid. You shouldn't feel like I haven't thought about what you said, I elaborated it because for me it's important to know I'm able to do it and even more important to let you know I'm able to do it. When I see a film where children are suffering because they are mistreated, I feel sad. I saw a movie yesterday where a child was forcibly separated from his mother and when the child found her mother again I felt a great emotion ... but then I stopped ... do I cry because I'm sad or because I like children?'

'Perhaps there isn't all that separation', replied the analyst, 'maybe you initially want genuinely to give love and protection to an abandoned child, then the attraction towards him insinuates itself and you get scared'.

'The way you speak makes my feelings appear good [silence] ... Nothing comes to mind [silence] ... Only that when I was a little child I couldn't sit on my mother's lap because she suffered a hernia and I used to think I'd break her with my weight.'

A silence follows where the analyst feels moved as she remembers when Marco told her he felt like hugging himself.

'Is this because you were never hugged?' she asks herself and him.

The session continues leaving the analyst with a disgustingly sweet-sour taste of undigested things, fragments of thoughts landed in her countertransference. She has the impression that Marco is happy to be back in analysis but that he is also somehow contemptuous of the analytic work. She has the image of him whimpering while watching a film but unable to be with a child who is crying and at the same time she has the disturbing feeling of having been herself unable to stay with a crying child during the session. She knows she feels angry.

'He doesn't want to feel he's happy to come', says the analyst to me, 'he can only be happy to have seen the problem, not to meet me again. The problem is there, I am not [adds the analyst with passion] ... everything becomes normalised and whatever I may say it translates into me being a weak mother who wants the child to grow fast because I break if I hold children, they're too much of a weight for me. If they want to be embraced they must bring me thoughts already elaborated, they must be adults, I don't tolerate children. I know that but am not able to give him back these feelings, I'm afraid of being too bitter and as a contrast I become too sweet and yet I know I do not stay by the crying child!'

Commentary by Laura Tognoli

I believe that only in the transference can we explore and live through the peculiar relation Marco has established with his own mother. She has been deprived of any maternal attribute and transformed into a 'wonderful adoring friend' completely dependent on Marco who can tell her everything without being judged, if anything always feeling wise. For his mother, Marco is always 'the voice' that knows what is good and bad for himself and for her. Marco asks his mother to read what he writes to his favourite teenagers, tells her how he would want to love them and he always gets from her the same response: 'You're ever so good!'

Going back to the session, I think I would get him to see that when he arrives he places all his things on the desk like a lawyer that must go to visit a prisoner and then, when he leaves, he picks them up again exactly in the same state as they were before. Is it the same with his thoughts?

On his way to the couch he slips but he picks himself up immediately, quickly reassuring the analyst that he is happy to have had the opportunity to come to know her. Yet if the analyst believes that he has missed her, she is mistaken. He is only happy to study the 'problem', leaving a snotty child who cannot become an adult and hug himself, the only thing he can endure is crying.

The really sad thing is that in analysis he cannot meet the mistreated child that he keeps as a prisoner inside himself. A child to whom the analyst's holiday has shown an internal movie: a series of images that talk of a child who suffers because he is separated from his mother. Maybe Marco cannot reach that child inside himself because as he watches this film he is full of doubts: what kind of mother will find the child who has been abandoned and is now a prisoner inside himself? Perhaps the mother-analyst who has tried to help and understand him? Or maybe the weak mother from his childhood whom Marco is afraid to break for being so needy? The mother he seduced by leading her to believe he is full of goodness, warmth and wisdom? Or the empty mother whose breast he has stolen, giving her in exchange his small and needy self?

In this session, the motherless child has found a dangerous Marco, disguised as mother, that wants him to grow up fast, wants him to hug himself, do everything by himself: a child disguised as an adult that the Marco-mother would love with all her-his passion.

As we talk, I am reminded of the Hitchcock film *Psycho*, when the main character dresses up as the mother he had killed and then stole her identity; he becomes a ferocious killer and murders the women who were, in his mind, the objects of her jealousy. When he is himself, he can have a loving relationship that unfortunately he tends to lose quickly because as he goes back into his mother's dresses and body, he is forced to kill.

I do not know what Marco's future will be but I know it does not just depend on the analyst. It depends on how much he has been able to preserve a desire for truth in this process of assembling and disassembling reality. This is the only thing that will allow him to see, through the pain of a wounded narcissism, the jealousy towards something he will never have, despite his desperate yearning for it.

The same glimmer of truth will allow him to discover that he too can give something nice and good that will never become someone else's possession, but it will remain his own, allowing him, too, a capacity to give.

He will have to go through a devastating experience of envy to feel the pleasure and beauty of gratitude.

Suddenly, during a session, I had a picture of the Italian word for 'disappoint' – which is 'deludere' and I saw it clearly as made up by two Latin words: 'de ludo', which means exiting the game, not playing anymore. I have always known this but I had never 'seen' it and above all I had never really thought that it is playing that allows the child to be a child with his or her great ability to imagine and learn through the experience and the illusion (in ludo) of the experience. A child unable to play is not a child anymore but a small adult devoid of the correct tools to face reality.

In the world of an abused child, a child invaded by 'delusion' (or disappointed, perhaps no more appointed as a child by those adults he had once trusted?), dies the desire to dream and play, dies the freedom to experiment his emotions with the security that there will be adults able to defend him from being what he should feel free to imagine of being. Dies the possibility to live the Oedipus in fantasy experiencing the power of love and hate with his very parents who are the main characters of the oedipal vicissitudes. Dies the possibility to see oneself as small and big at the same time: a child has the right to play with his imagination, passing on to the adult the responsibility of dealing with reality.

'Dad, when I'm big I'll marry you.'

'And I'll be the luckiest man in the world but I won't be the luckiest dad in the world and where will we put mum?'

'Mum will stay with us and I will be your wife and your daughter and we'll be happy ever after.'

This playful exchange in the language of tenderness, which I imagine ending with bickering, hugs and kisses, reminds me of the happy ending of a simple tale, naive and very distant from the complexity of life, but how it helps to grow and face Oedipus, holding the illusion of really living it and the possibility of dreaming of it!

Understanding and love are the essential ingredients to provide the strength to elaborate and overcome the Oedipus Complex without having to act it out in reality.

Oedipus was a child abused by adults intoxicated with power, unhappiness and fear. His parents did not speak to him the language of sexuality, nor the language of tenderness, they did not talk to him in any language. They left him alone with his ghosts, hanging off a tree by his feet.

Having parents afraid of life and death and of course of sexuality too, does not allow the exploration of what happens in the adult world. It is either all permitted or all doomed as sinful ... and of course the most sinful thought is imagining being hugged, kissed, touched by the parent you want to marry when grown up. When a need cannot find satisfaction, imagination always tries to possess that cold and distant reality, it wants to explore it, physically taste it, enter it, take revenge of it until a desperate desire to act insinuates itself inside imagination blurring the barrier between material and physical reality. Therefore, it is often very difficult to establish if an abuse has happened or has been desired by imagination: historical facts disappear, leaving black holes that blind the path of life.

★★★

'There is a lot of fog around me, I don't understand what's going on, I am confused, but in a ray of light I can see a slender, fragile, underdeveloped child. I feel I know him already and yet it is as though I see him for the first time. It is a child who has lost his history. He can't talk and I am afraid somebody may hurt him.'

The dream hits me deeply. It really strikes me how clearly it represents the weakness of a child deprived of the roots of his history. Our history, I think, is the only thing we really own – how can we lose it? And what kind of experience of our world can we have if the loss of memory of our past deprives us of a hope for the future?

But what really moves me is the fragility of that adult I am used to seeing as a sharp and cultured man, always composed and elegant, who is now lying in front of me on the couch, so upset he is close to tears because for the first time in 50 years, he is discovering something of himself he had never seen before. He had come to analysis as a man with no history, or better without a childhood. He had been a small adult isolated in his world where time and external events hardly existed or came to him as wrapped in cotton wool.

And in analysis, in the fog of a past with no memory, the story of a devastating solitude emerged, the story of a childhood spent in silence. Silence of words, silence of emotion.

It is a story that, despite my desire, is too long to tell.

I will limit myself to underline that silence, too, can be violence.

Silence digs a crack where the pain no one knows about can hide, a pain that, as time goes by, becomes impossible to communicate. Silence is a violence that remains invisible and that forces wounds to be healed before having given any possibility to understand how deep they were. It is a violence that slips away, that is quiet and does not manifest itself and that cannot become history.

References

Bion, W. (1967). *Second Thoughts*. London: Karnac Books, 1984.

8 When something that should happen does not
The unwelcome child and his psychic vicissitudes

Massimo Vigna Taglianti

Trauma: a long conceptual path from plus to minus

Current analytic clinical practice is paying increasing attention to the effects of primary traumas, generated by the checks or failures encountered while creating the first bonds with the maternal object. However, the advances in theorising about trauma – one of the cornerstones on which the entire psychoanalytic structure is founded – certainly did not follow a straight path nor were devoid of radical reversals in perspective, from the earliest theory of seduction, through the *Studies on Hysteria* and the *Three Essays on the Theory of Sexuality*, to arrive at the *Moses and Monotheism*, a paper in which Freud for the first time pointed at narcissism and narcissistic wounds as factors in the genesis of traumatic conditions.

Along this path of conceptual elaboration, which lasted for 30 years, a crucial turning point is represented by *Inhibitions, Symptoms and Anxiety* (1925). In this work, Freud definitively frees the 'psychoanalytic' trauma from the 'railway train' conception inherited from Charcot – who believed it to be a unique, external event – to arrive at postulating omnipresent 'traumatic situations' that are manifested in particular moments of child development. Effectively, the paper contains three theoretical novelties:

1 Significance is once again attributed to external factors as elements generating alterations in the individual.
2 Anxiety is recognised as an affective state and given the precise biological and psychic role of an alarm signal in the face of a danger.
3 For the first time, Freud assigns a central role in the genesis of traumatic situations to the ego's experience of *loss* and *impotence*. In conclusion, trauma can derive from external stimuli or from an excessive increase of internal stimuli; in both cases the ego is literally swamped.

Attributing importance to the various situations of *lack* and *absence* (loss of mother's love or of the mother herself, believed capable of protecting from dangers or relieving inner tensions) and reassessing the role of the death instinct therefore mark a turning point because they emphasise for the first time also the pathogenetic nature of the *minus* together with that of the *plus* (aggressive, violent and seductive elements that until then had been held to be the main components in causing trauma).

The unwelcome child and his psychic vicissitudes

In his 1929 essay, titled *The Unwelcome Child and His Death Instinct*, Ferenczi takes up these issues and develops them to the point of laying the foundations for a theory of trauma that introduces a new paradigm into the genesis of trauma itself: a paradigm that assigns fundamental importance to the role of indispensable organiser of child psychic development played by the *object that is present*; to the psychic characteristics of *real* objects; and to the relationships that – within a few years or so – would be called *object relationships*.

In fact, he writes that children who are *unwelcome guests in their own families* appear to have *observed* conscious or unconscious signs from their mother manifesting her rejection or intolerance towards them and so, for this reason, their desire to live is crushed (Ferenczi, 1929). The unwelcome child he is describing is not, though, an abandoned child. He is, rather, a child all alone, *ill-treated from the beginning* or *welcomed enthusiastically at the beginning but then 'ignored'*, because the tact, tenderness and enthusiasm of those looking after him have dissolved. Having become an adult, that child will reveal the salient traits of his character to be *moral and philosophic pessimism, scepticism* and *mistrust* but also an *incapacity to stand effort for any length of time* and an *aversion to work*.

Later, Winnicott (1958, 1960, 1963a) would express a similar concept concerning the deprived child (hated by his own mother even before he can hate her and understand that she hates him) when he maintains that this child's primary anxieties will be present and pervasive to a certain degree throughout his entire life. Ferenczi's paper thus introduces a chain of thought that focuses on the *sense of not existing*, an element today held to be one of the agents involved in the development of schizoid states (Fairbairn, 1940; Ogden, 1989) and depressive pathologies (Vallino, 2002), being associated with a maternal 'rejection' that can profoundly affect the individual, producing idiosyncratic effects that vary from feeling inhabited by a terrifying primitive sensation of virtually lacking anything vital up to a totalising 'order to die'. In fact, these individuals – sons of mothers and fathers afflicted by a *specific lack of enthusiasm for transmitting life* – structure their self according to an unconscious 'annihilating' logic (Meotti, 1996).

In this way, perspective about trauma totally changes, since it is in fact inscribed within an objectual experience that has nothing to do with *what took place*, but instead relates to *what could not take place*. It becomes a *painful negativising experience* that entails a splitting: a psychic *self-dismembering* that transforms the object relationship, which has become impossible, into a narcissistic relationship (Ferenczi, 1934; Bokanowski, 2005). The main effects of this narcissistic splitting can be summed up in the main as marring the process of instinctual ties; generating *psychic paralyses* or *stunning, pain* and *despair* associated with the introjection of an inadequate object; and creating a sensation of primary impotence, which can be triggered at the slightest occasion, capable of giving rise to transference passion, transference depression and negative therapeutic reactions that testify to the intensity of the psychic destructiveness at work (Bokanowski, 2001).

Consequently, we may postulate that the 'Ferenczian revolution' recognised the traumatic origin of those interpersonal situations characterised not so much by a sexual seduction exercised by an adult but by a *usurpation* — which is often unconscious and stems in turn from the parent's narcissistic wounds — of the child's nascent psychism. This is a subtle but potentially devastating operation effected by means of psychic *additions* and *subtractions* (an object that is 'too present' or 'too absent') that have profound consequences on the child's mental and emotional functioning, since they deeply and negatively affect the initial structuring of the primary internal object (Borgogno, 1999). In this particular configuration, the needs of the adult prevail over those of the child, who thus finds himself unrecognised and in the end negated. A similar event compromises the structuring of the mind and fuels those processes of splitting and dissociation of the personality that will become responsible for personality *fragmentation* and *atomisation* and for *identification with the aggressor*, which can all lead to the alienation of whole parts of the self (Ferenczi, 1932, 1933).

Winnicott's reflections (1949, 1956) emerge in Ferenczi's wake, postulating that the origins of traumatic vicissitudes are not to be found so much in the disturbing stimuli of a premature sexual excitation imposed on the child but rather in the absence of an adequate *attunement* on the part of 'a not good enough mother', whose inadequate *holding* and deficient *primary maternal preoccupation* would not relieve the child from a state of impotence. In particular, Winnicott (1963b) refers to those conditions in which the child is 'invaded' by environmental factors that do not correspond to his needs, and also to those conditions — which are particularly interesting for the point I am attempting to make here — in which, instead, something essential for supporting the subjectivation processes of the child him or herself should have happened but did not.

The case that follows typifies the relationship issues associated with the introjection of this powerful, unconscious *mandate to not exist* — a subtle but devastating form of psychic abuse — capable of leading a person towards a variety of clinical manifestations that range from a constant lack of enthusiasm for any investment to an unavoidable pessimism and desire not to live. In addition, this material illustrates the difficulties that we come across with these patients, who cannot risk exposing splinters of life in front of an analyst who has become, in the transference, the mother who hates him or her or who loves them only if dead (Meotti, 1996). Regarding their identification with the mortifying mother, these patients also attempt to reduce the analyst to the state of an alive but lethally resigned child, whose manifestations of vitality, like their interpretations, are systematically refused because they are perceived as bearers of a threatening change.

Paola and the curse

When Paola came to consult me, she was 40 years old and worked as a doctor in the most important hospital in the city, where the work rhythms and emotional pressures were truly astonishing. She felt totally unfit for the job she was doing and suffered greatly from comparison with her colleagues, whom she perceived as 'made of steel'.

In fact, since infancy, she had been pervaded by a profound sense of never being up to the mark, perceiving herself as 'a child who could drown in an inch of water'. At the moment of her first consultation, she saw herself instead as a 'retarded' little girl, who lived in a world in which she came up against insurmountable 'architectural barriers' every day that could be overcome only at enormous cost and effort. She felt herself continually swinging between a desire to be recognised as 'disabled' and the dread that everybody would be able to see the tiny frightened Paola – as though she were transparent – who lived inside her, maybe while she was tackling delicate medical situations where the patient's life was at stake.

To compensate in part for this invasive feeling of fragility, she had found in her husband – a self-made man who had redeemed his modest origins by sacrificing every infantile and irrational aspect – a 'father-master' who accompanied her in her life at the high cost of being constantly controlled and belittled for every single thing she did, so that at the end she felt even more 'branded' as being quite unfit for life.

She had already tried to do something about her all-pervading suffering, trying several pharmacological treatments and also psychotherapy, which she gave up after only a few months. She could find no reason for her distress and had the phantasy that maybe it stemmed from some sort of sexual abuse, perhaps by an old uncle one summer many years ago, although she was by no means certain of this and remembered nothing specific relating to it.

In the early part of her analysis, the narrative skein that introduced us to her issues of insecurity and to exploring her serious narcissistic deficit was represented by stories focusing on episodes at work invariably characterised by humiliations that she had endured at the hands of more senior doctors in the department or, during her times on call, at the hands of aggressive, domineering colleagues. She experienced these situations as deeply 'abusive' because, instead of receiving help and recognition in these difficult moments, she always received criticism and deprecation.

The first years of her analysis dramatically revealed that she was afflicted by what I called – paraphrasing the medical parlance that she often used in the sessions – a 'Vital Insufficiency': a sort of psychic 'shortness of breath' that did not allow her to confront reality unless with enormous effort and despair. Now feeling welcomed and mirrored in her suffering – that until then was the object of her stern, severe and belittling gaze that branded her as the bearer of a congenital incapacity, a shameful failure – inevitably led her to go beyond that painful anaesthesia (a 'pharmacologically induced coma', as she described it during that period) that had protected her for so many years. Her awakening was anything but painless, and the first dream she brought to analysis was highly emblematic of this: Paola was at a funeral and, on approaching the coffin, discovered to her horror that she herself was inside it, still alive but all scrunched up like a car in a scrapyard.

This horrifying *insight* into the coarctation and mortification that her self had undergone in her own life resulted in Paola deeply thinking about her story. She began to recall painful issues relating to the family atmosphere in which she had grown up, strongly steeped in traits of closure and rigidity combined with the specific natures of her parental objects. She began to remember the presence of a very authoritarian and terribly strict father and a depressed, irascible mother. The latter was even capable of not speaking to her for the entire day when she, a little girl, cried and begged for pardon for having committed some small bit of mischief. Her mother was literally capable of 'cursing her for being born' and, in addition, for having survived several attempts at abortion, since she had not been wanted at that moment, unlike her younger sister born a few years later.

The marks scored deeply on her from being 'an unwelcome guest' in her family impacted massively on varied spheres of her life, and this lethal saturation was only purified by a slow and exhausting work of 'analytic reclamation'. Paola began to remember that, after she had finished school, she had not chosen the faculty that interested her at university because she felt that she could not possibly have defended such a choice in front of her family, since it entailed moving to another city and living away from home: she did not feel in any way *worthy* of being able to make such an explicit request. She thought the same after her degree in medicine, when it was time to choose her specialisation: in fact, she would have liked to do psychiatry, but feeling 'maimed' and not 'up to it' decided instead to pursue a specialisation that at that time 'offered many job opportunities and was easy to get into'.

Sometime later, Paola recalled a similar situation when she was thinking about her marriage to Alfredo: passion was not involved (she had experienced that as a student when she had been passionately in love with an older doctor, believed once again to be unreachable for her); instead it was more of a choice dictated by the wish to leave home and by a series of 'sensible good reasons … What more could I have hoped for at that time?' Paola added disconsolately. Alfredo was in fact a serious and reliable young man who had made her feel safe because he embodied values that were very close to her own family's cultural background.

But even in her life as a doctor and a 40 year old, many choices and even small things, which for her were initially unimportant, continued to signal her profound suffering triggered by the mandate 'to not exist', or to exist but only to occupy the least possible amount of vital space. I will briefly outline the most representative in this sense.

Paola was employed by the department in the hospital where she works about ten years ago, immediately after finishing her specialisation. She has always thought of it as 'hell', but for a long time she never ever considered the idea of moving anywhere else, because 'at least there they know my defects and my limits … if I dared to go anywhere else to begin again I would feel like a disabled person'. During those ten years (and still for the first three to four years of her analysis), Paola had never been to the hospital dispenser to pick up the white doctor's coat tagged with her name and job designation, which the hospital provides for all its qualified medical personnel. Furthermore, she had never presented the necessary documentation to obtain the legitimate salary rise owed to every medical director after five years of service, and she had never managed to hand in the calculation of the hours worked overtime at the end of the month because she was embarrassed and felt ashamed of going to the administration office. For many years, she refused every scientific task proposed by her division head, believing she was not up to the task or anxiously dreading the moment when she might have had to speak at a congress. Last but not least, a curious aspect but, in my opinion, one that is highly emblematic on a symbolic level: it was only in about her seventh year of analysis that she felt justified to discuss with her husband the possibility of increasing the monthly allowance of her bank cash withdrawal card.

In our ten years' work together, analysis allowed Paola to view her suffering under another light and give a recognisable face to a conflictual and oscillating aspect linked to it, relative to the presence, on the one hand, of the phantasy of being incurable and, on the other, to the wish to give herself a *chance* to *exist* and to believe in being able to grow and recover.

On referring to this point, Paola's story and the peculiar development of her analysis allow me to shed light on some issues that I have briefly mentioned in the introduction to this chapter. I am referring in particular to the tragic reproposing – in the transference – of the interiorisation of the deficit of the parental investment and the re-emergence of that 'terrifying sensation' of lacking a psychic quality necessary for life, which I mentioned earlier when quoting Franca Meotti.

To go into more detail, in Paola's analysis the game of interpsychic identifications involved in the transference-countertransference dynamics played out in two main configurations. In countless sessions, especially in the first years of her treatment, I found myself personifying the child-Paola exposed to her mother's disinvestment: this happened every time she repeated behaviours charged with scepticism, recrimination and despondency, for example saying by way of excuse that she felt only suffering and that analysis was no help at all, since she was a desperate case; stances (both verbal and non-verbal) that at bottom implied an implicitly destructive psychic commandment along the lines of: 'Cursed be the day I started analysis'.

In the more advanced stages of her analysis it was possible for me not only to identify, but also to show her another side of what was coming to life in the analytic couple under the aegis of transference repetition; that is, the devastating effect that the interruptions due to Christmas or summer holiday periods had on her investment towards the analysis and on her life. In the past, these interruptions had produced just a few feeble protests but no despair, anger or aggression; now, however, they represented a terrible feeling of being aborted by the analyst's mind just as once she might truly, concretely have been aborted from her mother's womb. On these occasions, Paola was terrified that I would completely forsake her to the point of being infinitely 'far away' and totally disinterested and insensitive not only towards her suffering about being abandoned, but also towards her joys and her relative problems with the new activities that she had started out on. The latter – the absence of any revitalising recognition – was something that had such a disruptive impact it made her feel completely confused and disoriented in those moments, to the point of wanting not only to interrupt analysis but also to 'abort' the new projects that she cared about so much. 'I'm mad! What am I doing? Why on earth did I start out on all this? I've got to give it all up! I've even thought of committing suicide!' were some of the desperate laments she used to repeat in these circumstances when, in actual fact, she was dominated by a lack of trust or fear that I would not affectively support and bless her projects, but rather – like the internal object of her psychic reality – I would criticise them and, implicitly, 'curse' them. Stabilising these *vital parameters*, precarious and liable to considerable oscillation for such a long time, was the difficult and complex transformative challenge of the last years of her analysis, now concluded, which allowed her intra-interpsychic transit from identifications with 'abortive' objects to identifications with 'germinative' objects.

Conclusion

I have attempted to illustrate, through the presentation of a clinical case, how an early intersubjective relationship characterised by a powerful, unconscious *mandate to not exist* was able to profoundly and devastatingly influence the management of desire, the thought processes and the future interpersonal relationships: in fact, the deprecation and mortification by the object assume in this case the value of a real psychic violation that entails the emergence of those emotional states defined by various authors as *ego stunning*, the *agony of psychic life* or *psychic death*: a sort of freezing of the emotions; a mental functioning reduced to the *minimum* in order to survive by protecting oneself from pain.

The particularly pernicious and devastating aspect of this abuse – in the wider sense of the term – basically lies, therefore, in not allowing the child to have an experience that corresponds to his emotional needs, thus taking on the traits of a disorganising wound inflicted on the individual's subjectivity: a sort of *stigmata* ready to reopen and to advance again the original suffering. This suffering would thwart the development of a differentiated psychic existence even if the individual in the future would encounter people willing to welcome them and capable of understanding them, since every time the danger of the traumatic experience repeating itself looms into view, such crushing anxiety urges the patient to avoid any possible behaviour that might in some way lead to the pathogenic situation being reproposed, since the latter cannot be remembered because it has never been conscious, and therefore can only be re-experienced and recognised as the past (Ferenczi, 1920–32).

Taking up and developing this point further, Winnicott (1963c, 1974) in fact postulates that the individual will conserve and repeat traces of such traumatic vicissitudes, not because of the painful affects that were once felt but rather because of not being able to experience them at the moment when the traumatic event occurred. In his 1974 work, *Fear of Breakdown*, Winnicott describes most effectively how some individuals who might have experienced traumatic situations in the pre-verbal period – without therefore being able to psychically and affectively inscribe them – are pervaded by the fear of catastrophic breakdown. This breakdown is in fact dreaded so much because it has already happened; indeed, a fear of breakdown can be a fear of a past, not yet experienced, event. Winnicott's aims in this paper, by his admission, were

> to draw attention to the possibility that the breakdown has already happened, near the beginning of the individual's life. The patient needs to 'remember' this but it is not possible to remember something that has not yet happened, and this thing of the past has not happened yet because the patient was not there for it to happen to. The only way to 'remember' in this case is for the patient to experience this past thing for the first time in the present, that is to say, in the transference.
>
> (1974, 105)

Therefore, the trauma would be created on the margins of the non-portrayable, leaving behind, though, in the child's mind, indelible, latent, perceptive traces waiting to be given an affective even before a symbolic meaning. Every intersubjective experience will make the past traumatic impact resound, giving rise to an unbearable psychic pain. These traces will inevitably be reawakened also and above all by the relationship with the analyst, who must be willing to accept, explore and work through his or her own intrinsic traumatic potential to be able to offer the patient an opportunity for a new beginning.

References

Bokanowski, T. (2001). Le concept de 'nourrisson savant' (The 'wise baby' concept). In Arnoux, D. & Bokanowski, T. (eds), *Le nourrisson savant. Une figure de l'infantile* (The wise baby: A representation of the infantile dimension). Paris: Éditions, pp. 13–32.

Bokanowski, T. (2005). Variations on the concept of traumatism: Traumatism, traumatic, trauma. *International Journal of Psychoanalysis* 86: 251–265.

Borgogno, F. (1999). *Psychoanalysis as a Journey*. London: Open Gate Press, 2006.

Fairbairn, R. (1940). Schizoid factors in the personality. In *Psychoanalytic Studies of the Personality*. London: Tavistock, 1952, pp. 3–27.

Ferenczi, S. (1920–32). Notes and fragments. In *Final Contributions to the Problems and Methods of Psycho-Analysis*. London: Karnac Books, pp. 216–279.

Ferenczi, S. (1929). The unwelcome child and his death instinct. *International Journal of Psychoanalysis* 10: 125–112.

Ferenczi, S. (1932). *The Clinical Diary*, Ed. J. Dupont. Cambridge, MA: Harvard University Press, 1988.
Ferenczi, S. (1933). Confusion of tongues between adults and the child. In *Final Contributions to the Problems and Methods of Psycho-Analysis*. London: Karnac Books, pp. 156–167.
Ferenczi, S. (1934). Some thoughts on trauma. In J. Rickman (Ed.), J. Suttie (Trans.), *Further Contributions to the Theory and Technique of Psycho-analysis*. London: Karnac, 1980, pp. 216–279.
Freud, S. (1925). *Inhibitions, Symptoms and Anxiety*. S.E. London: Hogarth,Volume XX (1925–1926): An Autobiographical Study, Inhibitions, Symptoms and Anxiety, The Question of Lay Analysis and Other Works, pp. 87–178.
Freud, S. (1938). *Moses and Monotheism*. S.E. London: Hogarth, Volume XXIII (1937–39): Moses and Monotheism, An Outline of Psycho-Analysis and Other Works, pp. 1–138.
Freud, S. & Breuer, J. (1892–95). *Studies on Hysteria*. S.E. London: Hogarth, Volume II (1893–1895): Studies on Hysteria, pp. 1–323.
Meotti, F. (1996). Alcune riflessioni sull'inautenticità [Some reflections on unauthenticity]. *Riv. Psicoanal.*, 42, 457–464.
Ogden, T. H. (1989). *The Primitive Edge of Experience*. New York, NYC: Jason Aronson.
Vallino, D. (2002). Percorsi teorico-clinici sul trauma (Theoretical-clinical journeys about trauma). *Riv. Psicoanal.* 48: 5–22.
Winnicott, D. W. (1949). The ordinary devoted mother and her baby. In *The Child, the Family and the Outside World*. London: Pelican Books, 1964.
Winnicott, D. W. (1956). Primary maternal preoccupation. In *Through Paediatrics to Psycho-Analysis*. London: Hogarth Press and the Institute of Psycho-Analysis, 1975, pp. 300–305.
Winnicott, D. W. (1958). The capacity to be alone. *International Journal of Psychoanalysis* 39: 416–420.
Winnicott, D. W. (1960). The theory of the parent–infant relationship. *International Journal of Psychoanalysis* 41: 585–595.
Winnicott, D. W. (1963a). Dependence in infant care, in child care, and in the psychoanalytic setting. *International Journal of Psychoanalysis* 44: 339–344.
Winnicott, D. W. (1963b). The development of the capacity for concern. In *The Maturational Processes and the Facilitating Environment: Studies in the Theory of Emotional Development*. London: Hogarth Press and the Institute of Psycho-Analysis, 1965, pp. 73–82.
Winnicott, D. W. (1963c). Fear of breakdown. In C. Winnicott, R. Shepherd & M. Davis (Eds), *Psycho-Analytic Explorations*. London: Karnac Books, 1989.
Winnicott, D. W. (1974). Fear of breakdown. *International Review of Psychoanalysis* 1: 103–107.

9 May your steel be as sharp as your final no!

Gemma Zontini

In this chapter I would like to focus on how the most evolved aspects of psychic functioning (that is, the representational and symbolic capability) and of social bonds may constitute places to unleash abuse and prevarication on any subjectivity. In particular, my aim is to reflect upon the 'word' as a form of abusing, violent imposition of the adult's symbolic code on the child's psychic apparatus, which is necessarily vulnerable, it being still imperfectly established. Yet I would start by distinguishing between violence and abuse.

Language containing some form of violence is a recurring topic in the works of many psychoanalytic authors. However, I will here refer mainly to Lacan, Aulagnier and Laplanche, who more extensively dealt with the issue of violence in the discursive, symbolic order.

The violence of words is well stressed by Lacan (1957). He claims that the human subject cannot be represented either as an undivided totality (as an individual, even though this is an identity formula often used on a linguistic plane) or as being provided with substance. Lacan states that we are born in a language bath, thus introducing a conception of man, of the human subject, as a *speaking being*. The essence of being human is not individuality or a spiritual and carnal essence. The essence of man is language: the discourse, the tongue, the language spoken by those who precede us, identify us as subjects, starting from the first name imposed upon us by those who generated us. Therefore, the human subject is never an undivided totality but they are always subjected to the 'cuts' operated by the cultural, social and, most of all, linguistic symbolisms of the universe in which they are born. The subject, Lacan states, originates from barring the totality of the being, imposed by the symbolic order of language, by the signifier. Because language exists and comes from the others who always precede us and impose their word upon us, man is forced to give up part of its totality. We are born dead to life, as Lacan himself claims. In other words, what Lacan intends to stress is that man is forced to acknowledge their dependency on the other human, both as far as the randomness of existence is concerned as well as the satisfaction of their needs and wishes and the imposition of an order, of a law of communication with the other and the structuring of a social intersubjective bond. The symbolic action of language is what subjugates man into an order which transcends them (Lacan will later state that language is the true place of transcendence). But also, at a language level, there exists a separation between signifier and signified, between the linguistic sign and the contents of discourse. So, what is said (the words pronounced, the linguistic sign) may not coincide with the signified, with the contents of the discourse. For Freudian analysts such a statement is nothing but a record of the unconscious: what we say is subjected to our unconscious productions, as proven by slips, puns, but also symptoms, they too, in their own way, forms of symbolic communication. Much the same way, the human subject only partly coincides with the ensemble of signs, of symbolic representations which identify them in a certain way. In Lacan's words, the subject is represented by a signifier onto another signifier, is divided, is not an identity, it is not a simple presence, it does not consist of any substance, but its existence is suspended, deferred, removed by that same language which allows it to exist. This is Lacan's way of intending the original repression: where there is language there is a human subject, but it coincides with their erasure as a totality and is evident only as the effects of such erasure (that is, of its totalising individuality): 'I identify myself within the language, but only by getting lost in it as a subject/object.'

This means that the subject always establishes itself as being split (by the rules of communication with the other, rules which precede and structure its bond with the other), a division which disassembles its own structure and which eventually constitutes the unconscious.

Aulagnier (1975) also put forward the concept of the violent function of language. According to this author, from the very start of life the effect of the maternal and parental discourse (the mother as a word bearer) intervenes on the original activity of representation, which is sided by the transformation of the archaic functioning through phantasies. The effects of the maternal word coming first entail violence, the violence of maternal interpretation. Such violence is necessary because it shifts into the register of the utterable, of the representable what would otherwise be excluded: the body, the arousals and the external object receive from this a statute of internal representability and they constitute the subject's internal reality. After all, such shifting of the perceptive and sensory motor elements (in a more general sense, the biological elements) is the subject itself as ego. The representational ego is formed starting from this representative possibility of biology which is the foundation stone of man, as of any living being. If this primary violence is therefore a necessary condition for the ego to occur, its access determines the conditions to turn to symptomatic productions for those who are submitted to it, such as for example the primary delusional thinking through which the ego tries to reconstruct its historical reality and which cannot be left devoid of sense. A different way, a symptomatic way, to preserve one's own capability to utter, and therefore one's own existence.

In the same way, Laplanche (1987) talks about messages (though not necessarily verbal) circulating between the child and the adult taking care of them (generally the mother). These messages are provided with an enigmatic quotient, linked to the adult's sexual unconscious, which has to be translated so that the child may access the desire and the libidinal bond with the other human being.

Therefore, the word always imposes its violent action upon man and this process is one with the process of humanisation: human nature, we might say, is culture.

When does the violence of the word become abuse?

I will try to describe what in my view are the abusing drifts of language.

Words as impediments to translation

In my view this form of word abuse is linked to the maternal difficulty of being a word bearer, meaning the mother's difficulty to express her own assent to the original repression taking place. The maternal presence remains almost 'unuttered', the words brought by the mother are sparse; the carnal presence, dense with merging illusions, remains the core of the mother–child bond. In these cases the maternal word conveys rather the anxiety aroused within the mother herself by the possibility of a separation. Such anxiety, during adolescence, may take on the form of anxiety for the child's sexuality.

Vignette: G

G asks me if it is really true what she understood of the discourse of the other, generally her boyfriend. As soon as she says something about the other, for instance that her boyfriend lied to her or that he is not worth much, for one reason or another, she has to ask me if she understood well. She incessantly runs through the chain of 'objective evidence', in order to validate what she just said. Her subjective, personal thoughts do not seem to be of any value. An only daughter after six brothers, she has always been bonded to her mother through a love/hate relationship. Ever since she was a child, her mother has always asked her/ordered her to stay at home for long periods of time, even preventing her from going to school. In order to explain why it was necessary for her to stay at home, the mother turned to long and detailed descriptions of the mother's apparently physical problems, thus inducing the daughter to look at/consider the parts of her mother's body which caused problems or pain by saying: 'Look what I have to endure'. Yet these problems, so intensely described and iconically represented, did not have any clinical grounds.

G's mother, in fact, suffered from serious, acute anxiety bouts rather than from organic pathologies.

During her adolescence, as G herself would later say, her mother 'offered her to the best bidder': G must become engaged and then marry a rich man who can allow her to lead 'a glamorous kind of life'.

It seems that G met a boy who fulfilled her mother's wishes. But it is revealed that he suffers from a serious form of psychosis which affects his violent impulsivity, also sexual, and often it is G who has to pay the price. Her mother, however, urges her to continue the relationship with this boy. 'You must put up with it', she used to say to her, 'That's just the way men are'. After 12 years G breaks up the relationship. The critical moment is represented by a second abortion, strongly imposed by the man. At this point G finds the strength to leave him. But she starts moving from one relationship to the next. G never expresses any good reason for starting an affair, or any good reason for breaking it up. She gropes along amid physical complaints and objective evidence in the attempt to understand why a given person aroused feelings of love at any given time and why then the necessity to dump them arose. Her physical complaints seem to represent a moment of withdrawal in order to take a breath while constantly running along the chain of objective evidence, which may testify how right she was when deciding to leave somebody. Moreover, objective evidence also seems to be the testing ground of love towards the other: the other loves me, he will look after me. Objective evidence is therefore gaspingly sought after, reviewed and accurately assessed. And yet a doubt still lingers: did I understand well?

Apart from the elements of identification with the mother (physical troubles, more of a hysterical nature than organic), G seems to acutely show the deficit of her own subjectivity: no decision can be made starting from one's own feelings or ideas. Every action, thought, emotion must be provided with evidence: her psychic life seems to turn into a constantly ongoing scientific experiment. It seems to me that such deficit of subjectivity testifies to the malfunctioning of the original repression: the maternal word was unable to sufficiently convey 'the cut operated by the signifier', it could not sufficiently take on the representational function of body and affects, and therefore determine an aspect of psycho-physical continuity between the mother and the daughter. The maternal word has rather 'abused' the child by getting her used to putting up with the constant presence of the other, to tolerating the body (instead of representing it and making it the instrument of psychic desire), to enduring the bond instead of wanting it or refusing it. G shows a marked difficulty to recognise herself as a subject: her identity seems to be centred upon the support/enduring function. G supports her family and her boyfriends (always a little troublesome) and is, in turn, always seeking support: her partners must be well-off so as to help her whenever she is unable to get by on her teacher's wages, they must take care of her when she falls ill, they must follow and advise her through her choices. I would also hypothesise that the maternal word, which does not allow the subject to 'make itself' (as it does not allow either separation or access to the symbolic), opens up the space to its making within the body. It is from the body that G starts in order to separate: it seems to me that the ill treatment by the other, to which G exposes her body, replaces the 'symbolic cut' which the maternal words have not been able to produce and which might have guaranteed psycho-physical separation, body representation, symbolisation of desire and the bond with the other.

The word as a crypt

According to the theorisation by Abraham and Torok (1976), a crypt, a split and isolated place, is created for traumatic reasons within the psychic apparatus itself. The traumatic scene, together with the often contradictory libidinal forces which are part of it, is incorporated into a place of the ego excluded from the rest of psychic functioning, namely, a crypt. Incorporation is the main mechanism of this process. It activates when introjection fails, that is when the loss of an external object is not replaced by a representative, symbolic function which allows for its reception within the ego through its representation, together with the elements of drive which determined its importance for the subject. Therefore, when such mechanism fails, incorporation intervenes: it is not a dynamic, representative response but rather an economic response to the loss of the pleasure object. The object is conserved as if it were the real object, probably in its sensorial-sensual form, as a set of perceptive traces which do not communicate through symbolic and linguistic elements but which are silent and express themselves through languages different from the verbal one (for instance hallucinations or delirium, as in the case of the cut-off finger hallucination of the wolf man (Freud, 1914), a way to portray to oneself castration, not in representational symbolic terms but in sensorial, corporeal and hallucinatory terms). When the crypt is formed, the ego identifies itself, or rather, it merges with the pleasure object kept in the crypt itself. But it is an imaginary and occult identification/merger which must be kept secret for the ego itself. Only thus can the remaining part of the ego continue to function. But in this way also, the symbolic activity of the ego, in which words are also involved, gets fragmented. Thus the crypt becomes the place of the excluded word-thing, something which cannot be symbolised, a place which must signify that an (traumatic) event never occurred. Verbal language is replaced by more archaic language, the language of the body, of the organs and of the organ functions. The word-thing (with all its elements of sensorialness/sensuality) kept in the crypt cannot enter the continuous line of an explanation which entails going back to the unconscious elements, but it remains unaltered and unalterable. It trails back to its proto-verbal sources, to the archaic language of the body, of the organs and senses, it either appears as a set of images to decipher, like a rebus, or it manifests itself through anasemic translations, that is, by using phonetic assonances with other words from other languages or from its own language, all through fragments of sentences or words. It is, however, a word devoid of its communicative and symbolic function, as it no longer refers to the absent object.

Language, in fact, appears when the mouth is emptied of any object. The void gives rise first to cries and screams and then to words, so that the presence of the object can be replaced by a representation and therefore by the handling of its absence. The language which replaces such absence, suggesting a presence, can only be comprehended from the inside of a community of 'empty mouths' (Derrida 1976). This way the oral cavity plays a paradigmatic role in introjection as the silent place of the body which becomes 'speaking' only through supplementarity. One only speaks to substitute the absence of the object. The phantom of incorporation, on the contrary, realises the oral metaphor, preceding interjection, by introducing into the body a 'real' object: incapable of articulating the prohibited word, the mouth takes into itself the unutterable thing.

The word-thing in the crypt becomes a cryptonym. And the cryptonym, in turn, becomes the trace of an event which has never been present, a word-thing which does not constitute a word representation (of the Unconscious, of the Preconscious, of Consciousness). Neither a word nor a thing can be recognised in it. It is a sort of muted word. The aim of the cryptonymic word is not to signify, but to unsignify, along the lines of an anti-semantics which deconstructs any signification.

Vignette: F

F was referred to me by a colleague, a physician, a friend of her mother's. Ever since our first encounter I recognise in the patient a remarkably fragile identity, also in relation to her sexual choices. Moreover, F does not have any particular interest, she does not study and she does not work, she appears to be indifferent to everything. She tells me she has never been in love, but she has had affairs with both boys and girls, though without any deep involvement. Yet, since the end of high school she has been attracted to two of her teachers, a man and a woman both in their 60s with whom she has had intercourse, mainly kissing and caressing. She is always thinking of them, walking around the school just to catch a glimpse of them, constantly calling them up and often trying to meet them. She even spies on their movements and family habits. I link these two people to F's parents who were both already elderly when the patient was born; she has in fact a much older brother and sister. F remembers her parents as being very distant from her, because of their age. They were very controlling because she was the youngest but also because she would often fall ill, especially during her childhood.

When the patient is about 10 years old her mother leaves the father and moves in with a very rich and elderly man, taking her youngest daughter F with her. Because of their mother's choice, her brother and sister cut off any relationship with their mother and so the patient loses all form of contact with them as well as with the father whom she only sees at Christmas and for a couple of weeks during the summer. A few years after the separation, F's father suddenly dies. The patient says the event was not very painful as she never felt very attached to him. She is not really attached to her brother either. She has instead established a close relationship with her elder sister. She does not see her very often but confides in and tells her about her thoughts through phone calls and emails.

On our first analytic encounter F is accompanied by her mother who, before taking her leave, smiles at me saying: 'Please Dr, do help my daughter and let me know about the arrangements you will set up with her so that I can organise myself and accompany F to you. You know we live out of town'. She then asks me about the cost of the therapy: 'You know', she says 'F is my territory'.

During the analysis F will often say she is 'her territory', referring to her mother. Because she is much younger than her brother and sister, she did not have the possibility of living for a long time in the same house with her father from whom her mother separated. Therefore she did not enjoy the economic benefits connected to the presence of the father, as her brother and sister did. Her mother provided for everything, and considered her 'her territory'.

This phrase seems to enclose the abusive activity of the maternal discourse: incapable of representing the fertile ground of the discourse, F's mother conquered F's land, the new world represented by baby F, and she colonised it with her idealising projections. The maternal word sinks into the crypt where the trauma of a colonising maternal presence is kept. Trauma cannot be symbolised, as it is well known, but it can be repeated. So F, in turn, tries to colonise another parental couple. And as the ego splits around the crypt, the conquering movements onto the object/parental couple carried out by F take on the flavour of perverted acting out. It will take two years of therapy for F to define herself as being 'very down to earth' ('terra' in Italian also has a negative meaning, indicating a 'low' person), thus reopening the sepulchre of a traumatic discourse and from there the path to the symbolic and representative discourse.

The word as a mark, a sign

If it is true that language marks the body, the drives, the living being and the human substance, it is also true that this branding can break the signifier chain and fall into the psycho-soma. It is the word that gets abandoned, erased, abolished, and then it reappears under the erasure. The subject, as we have seen, is borne out of the other, in the other's field, it is identified by the other as a specific somebody, starting from the name. The word mark is specific, cannot be appealed and, mostly in a non-apparent away, is imposed upon the subject who gets erased, it is a sort of initial time for an operation of alienation. We might say that this 'branding' word constitutes some sort of enigmatic signifier which 'blocks' the onset of the representational-symbolic chain; it represents a stumble towards representation. And this goes as far as the construction of a psychotic delirium, which well shows the fragility of the representational capacity and the collapse of psychic signifiers.

In these situations language, and in general the representational symbolic element of the psychic apparatus, becomes a minefield, a territory which, far from being a protected symbolic zone, sinks its roots into the reality of the body, its perceptions, sensations and acts. Drive, self and body are intruded upon by language.

Vignette: C

C is a woman of about 50 years old, and suffers from a slight form of multiple sclerosis (benign). She is referred to a colleague of mine for analytic treatment by some of her colleagues. She and they are health operators working in a territorial surgery. The therapeutic referral seems to have been determined by the emerging in C of psychic symptoms: though there is no reappearance of the organic disease, C seems depressed, apathetic, at times ill-tempered, and opposes the new manager of the facility she works in. Lately she has even put on a lot of weight and is usually shabbily dressed. Sometimes she urinates while sitting and says that her condition has worsened (something which has been denied by her physicians). Her colleagues are loving and patient, the closer ones suggest she should wear incontinence pads, which she refuses to do. Notwithstanding her difficulties, she is very competent in her job, and though she does not acknowledge it, she has a good relationship with patients at the surgery, even serious cases, and shows a very caring attitude. She is very lonely, her parents have been dead a long time, her job is therefore the core of her life, it helps her feel 'alive'. The patient claims she does not want to get any analysis because, as she herself states, 'she doesn't believe in it'. Yet she has decided to take up on her colleague's advice because she feels 'weird' and needs to talk to somebody. She lives in a big family house with two cats and seems to accept seeing a therapist twice a week, mainly because of her loneliness rather than conviction. The analyst found herself thinking of an equation: two cats, two sessions.

Before this period, C used to go out with her colleagues and some friends, she went to the cinema, sometimes to the theatre or out for a meal. Then she stopped altogether: these things no longer satisfy her, everything is meaningless. Maybe, she says, she needs a man, but she is old, ugly and nobody wants her. C seems to be saying to herself: 'the game is over'. A depressive aspect? The analyst asks herself. In the past she had a relationship with a person the same age. With this person, she says, the funniest thing was 'massaging each other', and sometimes such activity took on some form of perversity. However, this relationship seems to have had friend-like aspects up until he decided to part ways.

On hearing this description of the relationship, the analyst thought that maybe it represented some sort of search for a soothing object, rather than the search for a love object. In any case, this account is related without any emotion.

C never talks about her physical illness, and she does not bring any memories or dreams into sessions: she only relates extensively about her patients in the hospital, she talks about practical things, of her rows with the chief doctor whom she finds stupid and superficial. One day something unexpected took place: during a session C tells of a long procedure for the physical containment of a patient in bed, because she and a nurse could not manage to find any other way to calm the patient down, even though she knew that this kind of procedure would get the chief doctor furious. He always tries, as much as he can, not to resort to this kind of intervention. There is some complacency in her account in which her body is in the forefront with the description of her movements, of the strength she uses and how she straddles the patient, the kind of tying she prepares and so on. The therapists finds herself saying to her, while imagining the scene: 'You certainly use very concrete means'. These words suddenly bring change into the atmosphere, the patient angrily clams up and says she wants to end the session.

What happened? The analyst asks herself. She feels she is groping in the dark, or better still she is taken aback.

C skips the following session. When she returns she remains silent for a long time. Then the therapist says: 'You seem very angry. I think it was the word "concrete", which was used during the last session, that stirred something in you.'

At that point C replies: 'Not really ... Or rather yes! I felt you were distant and judgemental! I already have a problem to believe in psychoanalysis! I'm not a concrete person.'

Analyst: 'Words too are concrete! Everything is concrete!' A long silence ensues.

Analyst: 'I would like to understand more.'

C. 'What is there to understand? You are a doctor and you should know that sometimes agitated patients must be contained. Full stop!'

Analyst: 'Are you sure you mean full stop? Probably you must mean a momentary stop. While you were explaining the scene I tried to imagine you [the therapist again recounts the scene to the patient using in this version a very plastic modality which mainly highlights the bodily aspects and her movements].'

C. 'So you were listening to me ... Well, after your words another scene sprang to mind.'

Analyst: (encouragingly): 'Oh good, another scene ... Where are we going now?'

C. 'It's weird, I never get scenes, very few memories, no dreams ... What is there to dream about? But it came to mind ... I must've been about 5 or 6, I was very happy that my father was taking me with him for the whole afternoon: he wanted me to try horse-riding. We went to the stables ... I was happy and excited. At the start it is difficult to get on a horse, you're afraid. But once I was on the horse and I found my position, with the instructor's eyes on me, I started screaming towards my dad, I was all excited: "Look, look!" I was reclining on one side, I wasn't riding straight, because you don't get your balance straightaway and my dad said: "Very very good". But then in a lower voice I heard him say: "You look like a sack of potatoes". Needless to say, I never went riding again.'

The paternal words, 'sack of potatoes', branded C down into her very body, down to the somatic illness participating as a psychic component. The other's (the father's) absolute power represented by the power to identify another subject (the daughter) in a certain way manifested itself in words which have functioned not from the point of possible representation of the trauma of the new, different but possible use of the body which can be represented and symbolised, but from the point of executing the traumatic abuse. There followed the condemnation of a bond with the body, almost impossible to symbolise and represent, therefore deprived of desire, devoid of the bond with the other, sinking deep into a physical illness forced to the contact with the not-human (cats, though fortunately, because she has at least been able to recuperate some form of bond with pets). Forced towards acts, forbidden towards symbols.

C continued with the therapy for a few years, even with some beneficial effects: the resumption of some kind of friendship bond, more serene relationships with her colleagues, one or two out-of-town holidays.

But her analyst learned, a few years after the termination of the therapeutic treatment, that the patient had suddenly died. Sentence served?

References

Abraham, N. & Torok, M. (1976). *Il verbario dell'uomo dei lupi*. Napoli: Liguori, 1992.
Aulagnier, P. (1975). *La violenza dell'interpretazione*. Rome: Borla. 1994.
Derrida, J. (1976). 'F(u)ori. Le parole angolate di Nicolas Abraham e Maria Torok'. In N. Abraham & M. Torok (Eds), *Il verbario dell'uomo dei lupi*. Napoli: Liguori, 1992, pp. 47–97.
Freud. S. (1914). *Dalla storia di una nevrosi infantile (Caso clinico dell'uomo dei lupi)*, O.S.F., vol. 7. Torino: Boringhieri.
Lacan, J. (1957). 'L'istanza della lettera nell'inconscio o la ragione dopo Freud'. In *Scritti*, vol. 1, ed. G. B. Contri. Torino: Einaudi, 1974.
Laplanche, J. (1987). *Nuovi fondamenti per la psiconalisi*. Rome: Borla, 1989.

Part II
Protecting the care systems to prevent burnout

The six sections in Part II describe various aspects of the work carried out by some of a help centre's psychoanalysts as part of their community outreach to assist women and children who have suffered violence, and to be available as a thinking space and resource for those professionals caught up in it, as well as for members of a help centre to think further about their work. The chapters can be gathered in three subgroups according to the group technique used with the caregivers: Rizzitelli/Del Favero and Naccari Carlizzi have led work discussion groups, Risso/Napoli and Pellerano/Pozzoli have led 'experiential groups', and Risso describes that kind of group work when she speaks of the group of psychoanalysts, while the group she led had organisational tasks as well as trying to understand what was happening 'beneath the surface'. With Stefano Bomarsi, Conte led a group according to what she had learnt from attending Leicester Group Relation conferences. Some confusion is unavoidable from the repetition, of which Conte has tried to give some explanation in her chapter. We have therefore placed Conte and Bomarsi's chapter first, then Rizzitelli/Del Favero's and Naccari Carlizzi's, which are more straightforward, followed by Risso's, Pellerano and Pozzoli's and lastly Napoli and Risso's.

10 All in the same boat

The activity of the Abuse and Ill-Treatment Group

Maria Pia Conte and Stefano Bomarsi

Maria Pia Conte

From 2009 to 2013 I have worked as a volunteer in a help centre for women in difficult situations. I realised that most women who needed our help were not happy to have to ask for it and were not at all sure that we could really be of help and not of harm for them.

They felt they could trust us only when they realised that as women, we knew we were in the same boat, intent in negotiating our course in a society in which currents and winds are definitely not in our favour.

Their mistrust was even greater towards the social services and was matched by a fear of even being abused by the services.

The operators of these services seemed available and willing to be helpful but there was a substantial difference in how they set out to meet these women and their problems.

Italian public institutions do not seem to have acknowledged either the Convention on the Elimination of All Forms of Discrimination against Women (CEDAW) adopted by the United Nations, signed and ratified by Italy since the 1980s, or the Convention on Preventing and Combating Violence against Women and Domestic Violence by the Council of Europe (Istanbul 2011), approved by Italy in 2013.

CEDAW recognises the ongoing existence of an extensive discrimination against women, notwithstanding the continuous efforts made towards an equality of rights. The Istanbul Convention recognises that violence against women is a manifestation of historically unequal power relations between women and men, which have led to domination over, and discrimination against, women by men and to the prevention of the full advancement of women, and makes a clear distinction between victims of violence of all kinds and perpetrators.

Single social operators are instead steeped in an institutional culture that presumes a theoretical equality of the genders and imposes a just as theoretical position of 'super partes' that prevents a realistic evaluation of the dynamics of power in conflicts between man and woman.

When in 2014 in the Genoese Centre of Psychoanalysis there was a suggestion to form a group on abuse and ill treatment on children and women, I considered it a very interesting opportunity to further my learning and experience on the subject.

Stefano Bomarsi

It is difficult for me to talk about the motives that led to my taking part in the Abuse and Ill-treatment (A and I) Group. They are rooted in my experience in working for two and a half years as a psychiatrist and psychotherapist in a prison in Genoa, a choice I had made with great enthusiasm and emotional zeal. In a very short time the enthusiasm, the involvement and the idealisation of the task clashed with a view that had become much more realistic and dramatic, if not tragic at times.

I met the prison as a total institution, imbued with daily violence, abuse and ill treatment that are manifest as an interstitial tissue that sustains and cements all the other tissues in a living body.

I met inmates, doctors, nurses, social workers and various personnel motivated to change an unacceptable reality, becoming slowly sick instead of with the same violence, the same interstitial abuse that soaks the walls and air of some places like the prison.

Giordano, a prisoner patient, told me how his capacity to dream, to transform during sleep, a concrete and violent reality was gradually exhausted until the dreams could not be anything else but an unaltered repetition of the repetitive, violent experiences of the day. That was how he could survive in that place, but, at the same time, he knew he had become an active part of it.

I believe I resigned in order not to take an active part in the violent dynamic, knowing that my role implied an unmistakable position of power. I also knew that I could do something only by getting out of that place where I had entered so intensely.

To take part in the A and I Group has meant for me an opportunity to try to understand and make good places of abuse inside and outside myself.

Foucault talks about 'no places' and during one meeting with a group of social workers the reality of such a no place as the prison, a physical space of abuse and ill treatment, was well described; that is, somewhere that really exists where it is often difficult, if not impossible to dream.

Carla, a social worker, talks about a working-class district in Genoa known as the 'washing machines'. She says she is scared every time she needs to go there; there is nothing but cement and decay. No green spaces, no shops, only a few pubs where shady customers hang out and arouse fear. She needs to go to visit some client in difficulty, but she feels that she is really afraid and that it is very difficult for her to enter that district. She has realised that she can face it if she goes with Paola, an elderly nurse who works for the same service. The place remains just as debased and dangerous, but with one or two colleagues it is possible to go in and work (see Chapter 13).

I think Carla and Paola represent very well the reason why I joined the A and I Group.

The Abuse and Ill-Treatment Group, Maria Pia Conte

The aim of the group was to study these issues and to share our psychoanalytic approach to them with other workers of the field through the organisation of different kinds of activities. According to our different training we organised work discussion groups, experiential groups and groups based on the group relation approach, which combines psychoanalytic and systemic perspectives. We also held conferences, training opportunities and so on. These activities are considered as part of the outreach policy, implemented in recent years by the International Psychoanalytical Association and shared by the Italian Psychoanalytical Society.

The group was formed by 12 analysts, nine women and three men, who eventually decided to meet once a month, with a representative and an administrative secretary. It gradually became evident that there were deep anxieties that made our working together very difficult.

I suggest two main anxiety-provoking issues:

1 The outreach policy meant coming out of the consulting room and the dyadic relationship between patient and analyst, and facing the multiplicity of the world outside, not as our private selves as we do every day, but in our identity as psychoanalysts without the help of the setting we are used to relying on. This means meeting with single persons, groups, institutions and negotiating our role and place in a possible meaningful relationship with them. Issues appeared along the axes of moving forward–withdrawal, superiority–inferiority and so on. It seems difficult to keep alive, inside, the presence of a potentially beneficial relationship when we are faced with others who have no reason to recognise it as such.
2 Trying to focus on violence meant entering a dismal area in human relations. We soon realised the group provoked in some of us feelings of being bullied, in others on the contrary of compliancy, the conflicts emerging could be met with denial or moral sanctions and so on. It seems as if coming in closer contact with violence functioned as a magnifying lens focused on every boundary violation that occurred within the group, in a way helping to bring into full light the place where the violent relationship had its origins.

These anxieties caused conflicts not only inside the A and I Group but also between the group and the managing body of the centre with conflicts along the axis of free initiative–coercive control and free speech–censorship.

These difficulties made us realise we needed help. We had a consultation with Mario Perini, a colleague expert in group relations, and we agreed to meet with him six times at a monthly interval. Stefano Bomarsi and I started the following two groups.

2014–15: group with operators from Genoa's municipality

We proposed three meetings to think together about violence connected with gender; nine people attended, eight women and a man, social workers, psychologists and educators.

Members began by talking about how difficult it is to relate with families where there is a story of violence, physical, psychological or sexual. They shared a feeling of unrelatedness, remoteness and difficulty in understanding the behaviour of women who live that kind of reality. 'Why don't they leave? They are collusive with the partner to the detriment of the children', and so on.

We realised how difficult it is to identify with those who put up with abuse and our wish to keep a distance, 'It wouldn't happen to me'. While analysing a sudden change of date I had imposed, we realised how, on the other end, it is just as difficult to identify with those who take advantage of their power, 'I don't do it, not me!'

Members began to talk about how often they feel forced by their own institution to act out violent impositions on parents or children to carry out a court sentence or a project decided by their unit.

We have felt how bad it is to be subjected to an imposition or to act it out and how often it can happen to dissociate oneself in the situation and to live it as if it concerned someone else, 'It's not my decision'.

Each of us, hosts and members of the group, had to recognise how strongly we try to resist acknowledging the dynamics of violence in human relations and how this denial fosters prevarication and submission, thus blurring the boundaries between us and the victims, us and the perpetrators, and questioning our motives.

At this point the group felt an unconscious hostile impulse towards the two of us that was expressed through a dream about some thieves that had taken away their documents and their car. We were experienced as those who were robbing the members of the group of their identity as representatives of an institution that, by definition, presume to 'do good' for their clients and of the possibility of proceeding automatically assuming to be 'all good, in good faith, with good intentions, super partes'.

2016–17: group with operators from small municipalities on the outskirts of Genoa

We proposed nine meetings to think together about violence connected with gender. Seven persons attended, social workers, psychologists and educators, six women and a man. All these people had taken part the previous year in groups organised by other colleagues (Rizzitelli and Risso).

They began talking about a mother who seemed at a loss and ineffective with her teenage daughter, with a totally absent father and a social service that was offering the family constant support, specific for each member of the family, with a temporary breach, in the help for the daughter, due to the absence of her psychotherapist. It seemed as if this momentary interruption in the support could swallow all the good that this constant net of human relations had woven.

Actually, the mother, with the help of the girl's boyfriend's mother, was effectively succeeding, by presence and persuasion, in avoiding that the gap be filled with an unwanted pregnancy.

We wondered whether we were asking this mother, social services and ourselves to dovetail with the illusory image of an omnipotent mother who is supposed to provide everything, forever, without making herself evident with her absence, in consonance with the image of a child who is constantly in need, never satisfied, who cannot treasure what he or she has received. Or of a child who cannot mourn the loss of a womb forever nourishing and cleaning, cannot face the loss of the omnipotent phantasy of being the owner of a womb that belongs to him/her exclusively and that he/she can exploit at will in order never to feel needy. A human being who cannot face the reality of depending on another for survival and comfort and cannot face the guilt of wondering whether he/she has exhausted her.

Then we spoke about a widowed father that spends his days in the pub with his very young daughter, exposing her to sexual harassment by his drinking pals. And about how difficult it was for the girl to confide in the workers of the children's home where she had been put in custody to protect her. Without a protective parent the whole structure of human relations gets subverted, adults become those you must distrust and it is very difficult to distinguish and recognise those who are trustworthy.

A man beats his wife and she is taken to hospital, the young child is brought to a children's home. We realise we are dismayed by the fact that the child is being placed in a surrounding unknown to him. We remember how up to now the children were left with the father, as if the violence could disappear by simply taking away the victim.

We think we feel a lot like that child, when we need to face violence and find ourselves as if in an unknown surrounding without protective figures. We need to count on ourselves to be able to choose and form what partial alliances we can weave.

An abusive man, who has received a restraining order, wants, at all costs, to be present at his children's holy communion. The children do not want him. The social workers judge the mother negatively; they think she does not do enough to convince them. Mother and children are afraid that father may make a big scene at the church. We wonder if it makes sense to ask a mother to press her children to face a dangerous person. The operators realise that in the father's attitude there is the assumption of the children being his possession and in the next meeting they relate how the mother has relied on the presence at the function of a group of mothers from her parish and is far less afraid. The father has come to church with a friend belonging to the military corps and has kept to the side without disturbing the function. When the mother felt understood in her intent to defend her children, she felt less alone, less afraid and could form new alliances. When the father felt the presence of protecting adults he arrived with someone who could help him keep within his boundaries.

The police have summoned one of the workers about a case of child abuse. On the phone, the police clerk was chuckling. Our colleague is furious; she expects that the police will not really listen to her, nor believe her and that her words will be taken lightly, minimised. We feel we would like to go with her; we do not want to leave her alone. We know how difficult it is to convey the reality of an abuse when we are alone confronting a culture intent on minimising. In the next meeting, she tells us she has been listened to, her words have been taken seriously and she has started new alliances.

One of the members, after being long in doubt, talks about a family where an abusive father has left home but insists on seeing the children. They do not want to see him and at the beginning do not turn up at the meetings that were scheduled with the presence of the operator. After some time, they accept to meet him, but the little girl does not speak and the somewhat older boy protests openly. The father does not understand why his children do not want to meet him and insists in going in front of the school and behaves in a loud and agitated manner. The operator does not know what to say to try and make the father understand that he must change his attitude. Words seem to be worthless. This man has a little flower shop and has won everybody's affection in his area; he cannot conceive that he is a source of discomfort and malaise for his children. Another member of the group says that faced with this kind of situation we remain without words, like the little daughter, and that they must be two very different languages.

It occurs to me that this difference is not only of language but also of the meaning and function of communication. This phantasy of possessing others makes me think of a prenatal way of communication between mother and child through the placenta. There is a distinction between the maternal placenta and the foetal placenta but they are so closely connected to be felt as a continuum: the foetus feels he or she owns this continuous flow of nourishment, detoxification and of biochemical equivalents of positive and negative feelings. This close connection does not need words and may represent a biochemical equivalent of projective identification. A state of mind to which we may massively regress when we feel overwhelmed with feelings we cannot cope with. This man seems to expect his children to fulfil this quasi-placental function: they must be there to allow him to draw vitality from them and to use them to evacuate the discomfort of his solitude.

In one of our meetings I made a mistake and arrived half an hour late, convinced that it was the real time of the meeting. When I realised, I apologised and asked if they could stay on and everyone complied. Going home I realised that I had confused the time of our group with the time of another group that I attend regularly. A group I love and that gives me great satisfaction, a choir of Gregorian chant. We follow our choirmaster in unison, in perfect harmony while we address our voices to an omnipotent god. I am an atheist but it seems evident that I would like this group to be like the choir, where an omnipotent master sings through us to an omnipotent god while we remain undifferentiated and without responsibility. Meanwhile, lost in my omnipotent phantasies, I abused my power in the group I co-lead, exploiting the dependence of the members while I was leaving them out, waiting in front of a closed door, introducing elements of superiority and disdain in our relationship.

In this group, each of us and together, we have to face, over and over again, the anxieties connected with our feelings of impotence, our concern of not being able to do our job well enough for those who depend on our protection, and the fear of having to face alone dangerous situations if we cannot count on a network that understands what it means to be afraid for oneself and for those who depend on us and have to try and build it as best we can where it is necessary.

In the next meeting, we talked about this event and realised how easy it is to be prey to omnipotent phantasies when we are faced with a difficult task and we search for some imaginary superior entity or we incarnate it without verifying his or her motives, pressed by our need to get rid of the feeling of uncertainty and of our responsibility in the results of our deeds.

A workshop with students of psychology

A colleague of ours, Rizzitelli, connected with Genoa University, has organised annual workshops to allow students to meet psychoanalysts on topics of their choice.

Stefano and I held a workshop on Differences in Gender. Fifteen students attended, eight females and seven males.

Well into the first meeting Stefano was talking when he suddenly stopped and said he had just realised that in the last half an hour only males had talked, irrespective of their role in the workshop.

We were struck by this take over and how effortlessly it had occurred.

We became aware that we had not even noticed it.

A few thoughts

We tried to make sense of the dynamics in the situations brought in by the groups, the dynamics in the two groups themselves, the dynamics with the institutions the members of the groups are part of or connected to: social services, the judiciary, the national health service and the dynamics in the A and I Group that the two of us are part of.

In a way, we identified recurring patterns, in particular, that discrepancies of power seem to easily give rise to bigger and even dangerous discrepancies.

Those who have some power, either because of physical strength or because of the role they hold in the group or in the organisation, or in society, seem to link it with a feeling of superiority, entitlement and automatic well meaning, that induces them to overstep their borders, thus invading other people's space, time and identity without asking permission. Most people who are in a dependent position seem to very easily comply with the invasion, trying to find good cause in the abuse, even against their better judgement, and thus augment the power and the sense of entitlement of the impostor (who imposes him/herself upon someone else). The result is that the private goals of the person whose power has been thus puffed up are substituted for the real task of the group and pursued instead. Those who object to these dynamics are very often felt as troublemakers and risk being scapegoated.

For example, in many of the families we talked about, the task of offering the children an environment that responded to their needs well enough to allow their development and evolution as individuals and as creative members of the family group was supplanted by the never-ending task of fulfilling the needs of the father, both of being soothed and helped in denying his feelings of impotence, and of being allowed to evacuate in the family itself all the toxic elements that derived from his frustrations.

This kind of dynamic makes me think about the cuckoo that lays its eggs in the nests of smaller birds and of the cuckoo's chick that as soon as hatched expels from the nest the host's eggs and grows to become bigger then the hosts who, driven by their breeding instinct, end up exhausted by the parasite they are raising. The wives of this kind of impostor are distracted from their main task as mothers and often the children too are enlisted as supporters and deprived of their childhood. These men in their regression to quasi-placental expectations seem to appeal to a breeding instinct that as humans we certainly have and that is represented in our omnipotent phantasy as the imperative to be needed.

In our experience in the A and I Group we realised that our training as analysts does not make us immune to this kind of dynamic, and this is irrespective of gender. On the contrary, it makes it easier for us to tune in with the most primitive aspects of our communication and raises the risk of being distracted from our task. This distortion seems particularly relevant in a group that has operational tasks because as analysts we are trained specifically not to act in our profession. But our training, eventually, allows us to get in touch with our discomfort and hopefully encourages us to seek specific training in the field of understanding what happens in groups, organisations and institutions.

11 Abused children
Reflections on the model

Renata Rizzitelli and Carola Del Favero

This is the summary of an experience with a group of social workers, spanning one year and a half, about the specific theme of violence. Our meetings took place in the Genoese Centre of Psychoanalysis and their leaders were Renata Rizzitelli and Carola Del Favero.

The caregivers' request was to examine the theme of violence from a more involving point of view, placing themselves under scrutiny through group meetings to face the difficulties due to the great emotional distance between themselves and the 'cases' they handled. Their aim was also to deal with the theme of the 'emotional costs' caused by their trench work in such difficult situations.

We built a kind of 'life preserver' in the first stage of our meetings; its intrinsic content was the possibility to refer to a common language and working field. This could facilitate the shift from a 'learning' and 'training' mental context, to an intimate, direct and involving group interaction, thanks to the possibility of sharing their personal experiences.

The difficulties of the caregivers in trusting us surfaced and so did their uncertainty about shifting from a 'didactic' training to a dimension that let them bring themselves, too, into play and enter a 'three-dimensional' perspective. Shifting would enable them to cope better with the dynamics linked to violence, so present and many-sided in their daily work, with a thousand faces and aspects. The third dimension allowed the group members to use a probe, the insight, to access 'deeply' the feelings triggered by violent situations; it allowed them also to focus on unknown contents about intra- and interpersonal, as well as transgenerational, relationships.

A feeling of utter loneliness surfaced, caused by their 'facing enormous loads, alone', unsupported by their reference organisations. It was difficult to share a working network with the other organisations, to feel part of a reassuring network, functioning, alive.

The group work was very difficult, from the start. During its first stage, the members expressed a resistance to their own experiences and phantasies and asked us for answers and protocols for intervention. In other words, 'prescriptions', to prevent them from asking themselves too many questions. For this reason, we always tried to focus on anxiety and to understand where it stemmed from.

One group member started a very important exploration area, bringing a phobia that had gripped her at the time. Now and then, she had been looking after her brother's young daughter, and she had always done it with pleasure and ease; however, a rising fear of losing the girl in the street had invaded her. One evening she was taking the girl back to her house when suddenly, as the evening grew darker and darker, she felt such a deep anxiety that she phoned and asked a family member to meet her in the street.

The theme of 'losing the inner child' helped the group to get hold of a fact: their profession had and has potentially damaging aspects for the caregivers, too; darkness, not knowing, however, only increases the damage.

This happens because trauma can traumatise also caregivers who get close to those who have experienced it; in subtle ways, often unperceived, it can penetrate deeply into their minds. It seeps into the setting creating ghosts, rather than the fruitful unconscious phantasies. The 'grammar of trauma' raises the problem of a rough sailing and of an equally rough landing towards the indispensable narrative dimension, a bridge necessary to elaborate the trauma itself.

Getting close to such complex and pathological situations poses the risk of being 'trapped'.

The mental setting is fundamental to avoid the risk of confusing or fusing ourselves with our patients.

The mental, as well as logistical setting, is a real anchorage; for instance, it helps contain the anxiety aimed at finding simply a scapegoat or at favouring, quite unconsciously, both silence and untrue disclosures, particularly with minors. The attempt to keep a distance, to turn away quickly from a complex and distressing working field, is due to the anxiety caused by standing in an area where there is no shelter, not even for the weakest and the most unprotected. A serious fracture of the basic trust can therefore occur – the fall of the gods – and so we can lose our trust in ourselves and in the other human beings.

At that time, the group member who had told us of the sudden phobia of losing her niece abruptly mysteriously disappeared from both the group and her working place. Obviously, she was going through a serious crisis, caused by dealing directly with her personal involvement with issues that break all rules and taboos and threaten to undermine the 'basic trust'. She found no other solution than disappearing to avoid losing the most sensitive and fragile parts of herself.

Another source of anxiety, besides working in such a difficult and distressing environment, was the clear indication that these working areas are also dangerous from a physical point of view.

In powerful voices, the members could then speak of the terrible cases when serious threats, caused by mafia-like dynamics, had been uttered to them. Official rules and regulations were swallowed up and alienated by other, wild laws, ruled by confusion and perversion: a state inside the state.

In this regard, we clearly saw how crucial is a firm 'mental setting', which should be carefully supported with the aid of protocols for intervention and institutional tasks well defined, clear and shared with the working group. We also saw that, in these settings, the caregivers could work with their minds only if they felt effectively protected, from every point of view.

The frame of a good institution and network organisation gives them the opportunity to use a healthy superego function, or, perhaps rather, a regulating fatherly function, allowing them to carry on with their work with the support of the institution and of the working group.

At the same time, we finally pointed out and accepted the risk of the delusional hope, from the caregivers, that a 'user manual' is sufficient to dam the strong emotions stirred up by this kind of work. A good frame is crucial, but not sufficient; it can be a prerequisite to start work in such complex and risky settings with a hope of doing something better for the persons who turn to us for help. We believe these delusional expectations to be directly linked to their resistance to thinking that they, too, perhaps, need a cure, individually and not only as a group. They were not rigidly separated from their patients, after all; they, too, needed a cure!

Accepting their anxiety allowed the group members to open up. They could trust us because they felt understood, accepted and they shared their emotions. Therefore, we could make room for and listen to their emotional issues and their deep, profound grief.

'Lost parts'

A meaningful and peculiar aspect of the clinical material was, in our opinion, the frequent presence of 'lost parts'. One caregiver describes a case 'nobody wanted to lay hands on', realising that she never collected information about the patients she had in charge. She lost their phone numbers and never remembered to ask for them again, although she had the opportunity to do so.

Another group member tells us that, during a consultation, the family member who had been harassing his family with his violence was waiting outside the consulting room in a threatening way, loading the atmosphere in the room with anxiety. The other group members strongly supported this feeling. During the first stage of our meetings, we watched together a film about the theme of violence (The White Ribbon, by M. Haneke). One caregiver told us that she had lost parts of the film and had had to watch it again, to piece the plot together. A sort of 'gate effect' comes into play when the contents are too loaded with anxiety and anguish; the mind can no longer absorb them and shuts down, losing some parts of the trauma plot. One caregiver says that, going over the notes taken during meetings with victims of violence, he realised that some parts, often the most painful, had been scotomised, had disappeared from his mind. Another group member adds that sometimes there is no room in your head for all the horror. The others agree and relieve their feeling of guilt caused by the inability to 'hold everything together' and do their work at best ... sometimes it is just impossible to overcome the defences linked to omnipotence and generated by toil and trouble. Some emotional contents are lost, cannot be let inside, are evacuated and removed from consciousness because they are unbearable.

Together we reflect upon these difficulties for a long time. Then something happens. A caregiver tells us of a dream she had the night after the group meeting. A wild animal burst into a scene of apparent domestic peace and pounced on her, aiming at her eyes, to blind her. She tried to get free, but here, somehow, her dream ended. Stories of sexual abuse stemming from perverted oedipal situations surface, confusing and therefore blinding.

Another time, after a particularly poignant meeting, Renata has a dream:

> I was walking, carrying a very nice shoulder bag. Walking, however, became increasingly difficult and my bag became so heavy and full to overflowing, that I had to carry it with both hands and hold it in front, while I could barely walk. My bag had turned into something like a protruding, pregnant belly. Then two garden hoses appeared, sprouting liquid, sticky mud over the bag, but over me, too; the stuff was sticking to me, making me feel dirty and unrecognisable. The trouble and toil to protect my bag and its contents were increasing.

Wild animals and garden hoses suddenly taking a life of their own are both violent, blinding forces that cover in liquid, sticky mud the vital parts inside the bag that are struggling to avoid destruction.

You can feel the trouble, toil and precariousness of the caregivers to hold everything, and themselves, together, to go on with their work, with themselves and their patients. These meanderings of the mind carry a deep anxiety, so that omnipotent aspects, magically successful at eliminating grief, come into play. You come close to situations when the parents, 'mother and dad', are meaningless terms because they are the opposite of what they should stand for; in the children's minds, they do not stand for care, shelter and safety, but for the reverse. The group express their magical solution, 'resettling children in safe houses, removing them from their families'. However, this is often performed in an equally violent way; it is no more than a fight or flight reaction, to get away quickly from the nightmare of reality.

Their deepest and most frightful anxieties can surface by sharing their experiences with the group, trying together to speak and contain everything and creating an affective setting. Dreaming their anxiety is possible, then feeling it, giving it a name, letting it back into the room, because they are feeling less lonely. It is possible to restore a viable 'psychological setting', whose ecological balance has been so seriously jeopardised and troubled by feelings of annihilation and uselessness.

This endorses the need for a working network since, as the caregivers become aware of the internal and external risks, they are afraid of the future, that is, of what will happen at the end of the group meetings. With 'risk', we mean also the danger for the caregivers who are in daily contact with such utterly destructive situations. They can raise defences against grief to protect themselves; they can adopt defence mechanisms against grief: denial, collusion, underrating or even failing to see … all that, with the contribution of the concerned parties, who sometimes try to manipulate reality to their advantage. We speak about the possibility to adapt, to sink into a gradual inner corruption and get addicted to the hideous, just to manage to carry on.

The difficulty to cope with such emotionally involving situations can easily lead to 'acting'. For instance, doing more than required by the caregiver's specific role. These actions can be the expression of an evacuating movement in cases that bring too much anxiety, a strategy to avoid the anxiety they cause. We can match another defence mechanism, of a narcissistic kind, to the former: the role of narcissism sometimes preventing the caregiver from realising that he has been manipulated or that he blundered. This can prevent him from reconsidering the situation and finding suitable solutions, effective in protecting the weakest, the victims.

Feeling defenceless, weak and unprotected generates anger, a feeling of invasion, contradictory feelings of omnipotence and fear, ranging from being detached, in an omnipotent way, to creating opposite situations of extreme closeness, of identification with the victim. In these situations, we can become fearful and powerless.

It is clear that we must take care of our mind. The group experience allowed us to see that the psychoanalytic thinking, with its intrinsic ability to explore and to know, can give access to a mental setting capable of coping with and containing very deep anxiety and anguish.

Having a place to express our fears, anxiety and experiences, both conscious and unconscious, provided us with a mental home where we could meet, all together, share our experience and deal with it, but also understand, work and grow together.

12 'I am naked, not just barehanded!'

Maria Naccari Carlizzi

I chose the title 'I am naked, not just barehanded!' to describe my experience as the leader of a group of caregivers who work with abused children. This desperate scream was 'thrown' to the group by an exasperated social worker, for us to understand his feelings, after working for years with victims and abusers, with all kinds of mistreatment and abuse. This sudden and violent communication is an example of what can happen when you are working in close contact with violent situations: you can become a violent, primitive person. Social workers, psychologists, educators, child neuropsychiatrists stand in the front line, on the territory, listening to ghastly stories of abuse that ask for, or rather, insist on immediate action and impossible compensation. Their emotional load is huge, often unmanageable.

This cry for help was immediately 'adopted' by the group, who, coasting along that powerful communication, could begin to get in touch with the feeling of being exposed, powerless and robbed of their usual working tools: naked and barehanded. Nothing left to protect them from the violence of these situations.

I chose to start the group that I led in the Genoese Centre for Psychoanalysis, asking them to share their situations at work. I asked the group some questions, to try and think about them together and begin a common reflection:

Why did you choose to speak about this case?
What does it move inside you and inside us?
Who is bearing the pain?

A reflective space was born almost at once in the group, as we tried to find answers together. This allowed us to undergo a first transformation: something hard and indigestible could turn into something thinkable.

One member brings an image to the group, how he was feeling towards the cases of violence and abuse, describing himself thus: 'The stone grinder breaks down, after a while.'

If you are grinding by yourself the heavy rocks of abuse, if you cannot think together, if you cannot start any transformation, what is left are stones that we cannot think about but only grind, if possible.

Therefore, we try to find shelter, we stiffen and use defence mechanisms, as dissociation, denial, splitting, negation, concretisation, a tendency to acting out, but also insensitivity, cynicism, resignation, weariness. The group adopts the image of the 'stone grinder' that thoroughly describes how they are feeling and the psychic defences employed. However, even a stone grinder will break down or wear out. Eventually, their emotional load will get unmanageable and there is a deep and painful urge to change their job. Psychosomatic symptoms often appear, such as headaches, backaches, fever, widespread pain ... they can be deciphered in the group, which often causes unexpected recoveries.

The stones are harmful; they cannot be digested, less so metabolised. The group and the opportunity of sharing and empathy derived from their common experience enables them to elaborate pain, their own pain or pain projected by the other members. They can share their experiences of impotence, uselessness and anger and foster new hope. Thanks to these elements they can proceed, from stone grinding to the thinkable.

When the feelings turn into thoughts, the psychic defences take the shape of phantasies that offer psychic shelter, where you can sometimes pause.

One member says, 'When I go on home visits to those God-forsaken places, I often think of a mountain pond and stop there for a while.' Getting away from reality does not help to cope with it and can even worsen things, can make you ill. When the going is uphill, a stop can help, if it does not turn into a permanent stay; quite different are the flights from a reality that is too harsh to face, bordering on idealisation.

We discuss responsibilities, 'faults': 'This would not have happened ... once, when the centres for health and social services were working! ... This is the politicians' fault, not ours! We are few, getting fewer and fewer!'

There is a deep understanding in the group about how you feel when you must cope with these issues every day. The painful awareness that exposing yourself is necessary, like it or not, surfaces and is shared; they must lend their vital energy and provide people, who have lost all their bearings, with a meaning to their lives. About this, a caregiver tells us that a mistreated woman told him: 'Do not bother about me, there is nothing to do; my mother was beaten, too, and when she reported my stepfather, she was beaten even harder!' We can speak about how we feel when we are dealing with peculiar situations, where the victims, robbed of their self-confidence and of their ability to complain, paradoxically feel harassed by our offer of help.

The group, thanks to its unconscious dynamics, allows its members to expose themselves and face the astonishment at being robbed of their own emotional resources by the very patients they are trying to help. The theft is undercover, through mainly unconscious or pre-conscious projections and identifications that painfully come to life in the group.

A dream perfectly reflects the group atmosphere. One caregiver, with great sincerity, tells us about a recurring dream he had: 'I dream that I am sliding away, on my back, unable to see or to understand what is happening! There is nothing I can hold on to.'

Another describes a recurring nightmare. It is about 'the robbery at my local baker's'. This feeling of being a victim of a collective theft gets worse whenever you cannot offer the very least, the smallest protection to people, as much as you wish to do so. You can live this conflict inside yourself or take it out against the Authority (the municipality, the court, the consulate, the head of the health or social services) who refuse to grant the money needed to set up these projects.

Many questions gradually arise during our meetings, through the emotional growth caused by understanding the implications of a daily contact with 'the bearers of pain':

Who listens to the loneliness of those who work as listeners?
How can you listen to yourself if you do not have the emotional time to do it, due to the heavy workload and the continuous hurry?

> You feel isolated, powerless: stark naked, not just barehanded!

Following a natural flow and with ease, one member presents the group with his reverie indicating a solution to survive the load of abuse:

> I almost drowned inside a wave as a child. In those brief moments, I understood that I had to choose what to do, or else I would not survive! Opposing it or drifting with it? I drifted with the wave and so it carried me back to the surface!

We remark upon this, in turn,

> You have to learn to stay still, before taking action. You must find the right distance from pressure, to see where it is emotionally leading you; a distance also from people who ask for your help, but, at the same time, saddle you with negativity. You need time and patience, you must learn to respect violent persons, too, or else you will become like them. When you are listening to some stories, you would like to do unto them what they did to others ... but you cannot ... Tolerance is necessary to protect yourself and your patients. To stand violence, you should be able to read its complexity!

Someone is voicing his anger at not being understood, not even by his colleagues, another is mourning the victim. 'We keep listening to human stories that undermine our sense of justice!' Someone else points out how guilty you feel in those situations when you could do nothing at all and how angry you feel for the scarce help from the service network that has done nothing to support and listen to the caregiver and his or her complex mission.

The caregivers ask for a meaning to their work, crushed between the deafness and authority of the establishment and the violence of the abusers. In this latitude, you can lose the boundaries of the self and of your role, you risk death, 'we can do nothing, they are mocking us! On which side is the establishment?'

The group shows anxiety for the scarce physical protection; they clearly point out that the operators dealing with violence and abuse have scarce juridical and even physical protection and that violence is like an infectious disease.

Even I, the leader of the group, connect with a remote memory:

> I was working in a centre providing health and social services. When the social worker removed from home a little girl, a patient of mine, abused by her brother, her father threatened us with his gun. We all feared for our safety for months and we wondered whether we were exaggerating or we really had to protect ourselves!

The group remarks that in these situations there is fear for ourselves and for the victims, the danger of underrating or overrating the danger signs, since fear can both be disorganising and, on the contrary, excessively activating. If the urge to run away prevails, as sometimes happens, and the caregiver gets shifted to some other job, this function fails and only scraps of their emotional experience will remain for them, too.

Conclusion

The group focuses on the caregiver's role as the 'witness of the stories'. These stories often span generations and the caregivers act as the guardian of memory, even if they can take no practical action. With their continuing presence, in time and space, they grant abused and mistreated children and adults the possibility to come back and find again something about themselves. The caregiver must be helped to think to endure. Enduring, for the group members, means not to oppose stiffly, but to remain alive and lively. They must look inside themselves for the ability to face unbearable feelings; to face what psychoanalysts call the 'Uncanny', reading carefully inside themselves and their working group the emotional reactions, both their own and projected by the patients, during and after their meetings. Going on with our experience is necessary, even if it entails pain, and we must recommend it as a permanent mode of work: reading the unconscious dynamics of the group, to bear the emotional costs of its members and help them to keep their role and their mental integrity.

13 Abused children, caregivers, psychoanalysts – voices from the groups
Reflections on the model and its use

Anna Maria Risso

In the summer of 2013, the manager for Project Arianna of the municipality of Genoa, a project for children, teenagers and abused women, contacted me, as the president of the Psychoanalytic Centre of Genoa. The manager is also the founder of the working network Amaltea, which includes the main city hospitals, the public prosecutor's offices at the ordinary and juvenile courts and the social policies office of the municipality of Genoa.

The Psychoanalytic Centre of Genoa was asked to sign up to the working network and make our training expertise available for the operators of the municipality of Genoa who were working, with different roles and in different sectors, with children, teenagers and female victims of abuse.

In the course of several meetings we outlined a project that should and could use the group as a resource.

In September 2014, some psychoanalysts of our centre – who, in turn, had set up a group – made this instrument available to the caregivers involved at different levels with mistreatment and abuse; I will try to describe below its clinical-theoretical features.

The same psychoanalysts who were involved in the caregivers' groups made a group experience of their own under the leadership of a colleague from another centre, an expert in groups and organisations.

Bion (1962a, 1962b) stated that we commonly say that if a person has a nightmare at night, this is due to indigestion, a somatic indigestion; we can, however, think that the nightmare is the effect of a mental indigestion.

That person has piled up a series of experiences and lived through involving emotional situations that he could not metabolize and digest.

The nightmare is the effect of the piling up: a person wakes up in the grip of anxiety, his psychic apparatus was overcome and could not digest those experiences.

When we dream, instead, our mind is trying to work creatively on what has happened and turn it into a new product, namely, the dream, that can be open to a later, further understanding. The groups that came to life could therefore become places-times to dream their own and the others' anxiety, to wrap it up with words, images, sounds and colours to talk about together.

Places-times homes, here I introduce a word particularly endearing to us all: home. In the practice of cruelty, human feelings are banished from home, squeezed away by a mind that is shutting itself off. Eric Brenman wrote of love modifying cruelty in the normal development; you must do something to prevent human love from working, to see the rise of cruelty. According to Brenman, a peculiar form of mind narrowing is used to enact and to keep enacting cruelty, for the purpose of totally removing any human feeling. Brenman (1995) used the term 'squeezing' to express the psychic operation enacted by a person who can become violent and cruel. Human understanding is evacuated, squeezed away. The consequence of this process is the possibility of enacting an inhuman cruelty. History teaches us, and the news keeps reminding us, that triumphing over human compassion and understanding seems to be a part of human nature.

What did we have to give a home back to, then, as we were getting involved? What were the caregivers in our groups and the psychoanalysts who were working with them in the groups, trying to give a home back to? The need to be helped, I think, the need for lively interactions with other human beings, the acceptance of our limits, the acknowledgement of the risk we are all running, since our job puts us in daily contact with pain, and such a deep pain, pain caused by abuse and mistreatment.

I am here going to reflect on some features of the group as a tool we tried to use at different levels and then I will go on directly to the clinical setting. The clinical material that I use comes from groups with the caregivers, led by the psychoanalysts, and from the group of the psychoanalysts themselves.

When I speak of a group, I mean a group with an analytic function, where we assume that the psychoanalytic function of the mind is activated starting from the data that we can directly observe in the experience made together, in what is usually called the 'here and now'.

A group, therefore, mainly and specifically intended as a situation that allows for the individuation and acknowledgement of the group phenomena, starting from first-hand experience. Such a group would give life, by its own nature, to a transformative and cognitive function, while the therapeutic function would remain in the background, although certainly not absent.

The contact with the institutional context of the setting is, no doubt, a key feature, strongly affecting the modalities of group contact and leadership.

I quietly introduced the adjective 'therapeutic' among the group functions ... are we then talking of a disease? What disease are we talking about? What covert disease is healed or are we going to heal? Violence is catching, so we wrote as an introduction to our group proposals ... is violence, then, the disease? Do operators dealing with violence, mistreatment and abuse run the risk of becoming, in turn, violent, mistreating and abusing?

What would then be the cure? We know that no therapeutic change aims at obtaining a painless life. We are well aware that not all the life contacts are necessarily pleasant: life is painful and enriching at the same time. Hate and love are both parts of life itself. All that is dimming, disheartening, muffling is instead contrary to life.

We should consider the groups with the caregivers as a kind of vaccine therapy that could grant immunity. In that way, the vaccinated/to be vaccinated operators could work in close contact with violence and avoid catching the disease of violence. How long does the immunity of the group therapy last? Do we need booster doses? Can we think of the group meetings as supplies – at fixed times – of the right amount of antibodies needed to fight off the disease, every time we catch it? A kind of serum therapy, then? What about the psychoanalysts?

I believe that the group experience allows us to catch the disease several times and be healed in the 'here and now'; we learn how to use our available mental and emotional resources, continually crossing and recrossing a specific, of that moment, schizophrenic-paranoid position to reach the safe haven of a possible, specific, of that moment, depressive position.

Thanks to the research of the last decades, we can now make use of an original model, correlated but quite distinct from the dual psychoanalytic model, for the group experience.

We can always ascertain that the relationships among members of a group are multiple, mutually simultaneous, intertwined and involve 'subjects who are, at the same time, objects, and vice versa'; besides, there are dynamic relationships in the group, among the members and their own 'set: this is defined as a transpersonal unitary object', shared by all members, containing the members, but contained in the mind of each single member, as well (Longo & Neri, 1985).

We can already find the initial construction of a new specific model in W. Bion's studies on groups (1961). According to Bion, the main issue in the observation of a group is that the working field ... (of the psychoanalytic research) change to include phenomena that cannot be studied outside the group. In fact, they show no activity in any working field outside the group. (Bion, 1961) A research started from Bion's reflections, to develop a model suitable for the analytic investigation of group thinking.

A research started from Bion's reflections, to develop a model suitable for the analytic investigation of group thinking.

I propose the model of 'the string cradle' to show an image of the kind of dynamic interaction typical of the group thought development (Neri, 1979a, 1979b). This game still retains a ritual and symbolic acting value in some areas of Oceania, Africa and by the Eskimos. A piece of string, knotted at both ends, is intertwined around the fingers of one person, taking the shape of a cradle. Other people then, in turn, twist the string round their fingers, obtaining each time a new network pattern.

The group work, too, goes on by leaps, a situation where the usual space-time landmarks are suspended. The group gradually develops a cognitive process, it structures an inner linguistic and space-time orientation and a growing feeling that its members belong to their shared experience situation.

The understanding in the group comes from the participation and from the opportunity to build up an intellective, emotional and phantasmal common area, that we can call the area of belonging (Neri, 1979c). All the group members invest, in parallel and simultaneously, upon the area of belonging, with fantasies that consider it as a dynamic space, allowing for an extension of the self of each individual member, as well as with fantasies that consider it as a space outside the self, an area of action and expression of the dynamics of the group as a whole. The setting up and stabilisation of the area of belonging allow for a functional relationship between the parts and the whole, and help get past the stages of lesser integration that may be present in the group (Neri, 1982).

We can observe repeated swings in the relationship between the group and the single members, corresponding to personal adjustments of the member participation between two focal points: I (individual) and G (group). These swings have a function of economic adjustment in the group: whenever belonging to the social set as individuals with distinct functions (position I) causes an unbearable anxiety, coupled with a growing feeling of a loss of the group identity, there is a swing towards fusion, depersonalisation, or rather, deindividuation (position G). When, however, being a group, working together confused (G) causes a growing feeling of oppression to the members, the functions are brought back to the individual members (reindividuation = I) (Neri, 1983).

The group processes what is contained in the area of belonging through successive transformations, oriented by the analytic function activated by the leader.

This can concern either materials or elements of thought that can be more or less evolved; the possibility of their transformation in K (cognitive transformation, in Bion's words, 1965), depends mainly on this factor.

This can concern less evolved elements that undergo a transformative process as well, enabling them to return easily in the field of the knowable experience. The experience itself would therefore be expanded, thanks to the rise of growing elements of thought.

With the aid of the clinical material, I will now try to show how this occurs. I will try to show how the group builds the possibility to cope, quite freely, with an emotionally loaded experience, self-determined, a possibility based on the collective contribution of its members.

We will always keep in mind, as Longo and Neri remind us (1985), that every Experience Group is crowded with parasite configurations, too; so will be considered any rise of micro pathological behaviours or any exaggerated or eroticised transference-type acting out.

Those situations will cause difficulties to the group dynamics and, when present, they undermine the possibility to maintain a constructive working level of the group thinking (working group, in Bion's words, 1961). Longo and Neri (1985) also stress the fact that this is even more important in the temporary groups, where the leadership should favour the re-individuation of the members within the time boundaries of the experience.

Our groups are temporary, meaning that a special time of one year, that can be repeated, is provided (October–November, June–July). The third special time is starting in autumn, with an open group (with a maximum number of members); the group is formed each time with the arrival of new members and the possible loss of the previous year's members. It has worked in this way, so far. Also, the psychoanalysts' group is open, any member can ask for membership. It gained a new member in the course of last year.

The group experience of the psychoanalysts' group was temporary; we are currently considering the possibility of starting a new experience.

After this general introduction about the group with an analytic function, dealing with the transformative factors underlying the cognitive processes in the group, we are now going to introduce the clinical material.

The clinical material comes from the psychoanalysts' group, from a few groups led by the centre psychoanalysts and from the experience group that the centre psychoanalysts attended. Their experiences intertwined and overlapped in a complex manner; I am here trying to bind them together and highlight the red thread running through.

Nothing has happened

A group member tells us that he met a friend of his, some years his senior, after a long time. He knew that his friend had fallen ill with a serious disease; he describes his friend as an affectionate, sincere, helpful person, to whom he had turned for help more than once in difficult times of his life. Their casual meeting takes place in a supermarket parking area; his friend is wrapped up in clothes that hide him almost completely. The narrator is sitting in his car, just going to drive out of the area; he is undecided: should he stop, get out of his car and say hallo to his friend? He has not met him since he fell ill, although he has often thought of going to visit him.

However, something has always kept him away and is keeping him away now: a feeling of unease and fear at the sight of his friend's frightful change, the idea of intrusion into a forbidden privacy, the shame of meddling into something that is no business of his. The very shame that his friend might feel if he is recognised and forced to show his pain and his striking change. The narrator drives away from the parking area and from his friend, not quite sure of the correctness of his decision.

The same night he had a dream that he brings to the group:

> I am in an eating house and I am going to sit at a table where there are other chairs for other people. I realise that my friend, the one I met at the parking area, is already sitting at this table. I am very surprised and amazed to see that he is in excellent shape, dressed as always. In short, he is again the friend I shared so many years of my life with, the friend I know so well, there are no marks of his illness.

The group begins to speak about the contact with pain, deep pain, which is difficult to get close to, a pain that alters people and their lives; a pain that very often is difficult to talk about, both for the affected person, and also for the person who should help.

The choice in the dream, as well as in life, can be just not to see, not to think and not to speak, denying such a painful reality, pretending that nothing has happened. The friend is still his old self, the abused child, the mistreated woman is still there, whole and unharmed, while a voice says: 'Nothing has happened.'

The washing machines are made of concrete

They are an example of urban architecture apparently aimed at answering the housing needs of that time in the area, but are caused by political and economic issues of profit. They raped the area, turned it into a ghetto. You cannot enter that dilapidated area, made of concrete, with no hope of green, full of danger and violence. Fear and terror hover over the group at the thought of going there. A few smiles of acknowledgement, silent agreement and suspended understanding floating in the air. Someone says: 'I don't want to go there, to enter that place. If I really must, at least I don't want to be alone.'

Entering abuse and mistreatment is like entering that cold, dilapidated area, but is it also a place in our mind, perhaps, where we are in danger of going through the spin cycle, thoughtless and hopeless?

The concrete of the area reminds us, our imagination, of the lack of colours and of emotional liveliness, the dominance of the emotional grey is the only possibility of survival in the reality of mistreatment and abuse.

There are no food shops, bakeries or anything else in the area. Just shutters, for facilities that never opened and never worked. Nothing in their place but dilapidated, deprived areas and a few wretched and sad-looking coffee bars. The image pictured by the group is powerful. The group is speaking of a place that it could not enter, so far. It is wondering why they must go there. If they really need to go there, then they must be helped; they cannot go there alone.

The group was born as a place of reclamation and of answers to need, but is afraid of becoming a dilapidated, ghetto area if it goes there. The washing machines never worked, they do not clean: on the contrary, they soil. Could the group, born with a cleansing purpose, become a dilapidated, dirty area? The group could become a concrete group, a concrete washing machine that does not clean, instead traps its members into its non-working and produces fresh refuse of its own.

> The enemy is too powerful, invincible …
> '*You say*
> Our movement is in a bad shape.
> The darkness is increasing.
> Our powers are decreasing …

> But the enemy stands stronger than ever.
> Their powers seem to have increased.
> They have taken an appearance of invincibility.
> We have made mistakes,
> it is undeniable.
> Our passwords are in disarray. The enemy has taken our words,
> and twisted them into something unrecognizable.'
>
> (Brecht, 2015, *To the wavering*, pp. 130–131)

The voice of a poet, Bertolt Brecht, rises from the group. The group is asking a poet to give voice to their feelings. Franco Fornari (1981, 1988) said that who is involved with people whose souls are suffering, feels that he must take upon himself a grief they cannot cope with. When we are enjoying a work of art, however, the artist takes upon himself and repairs our grief.

The group appoints a poet with the task of finding words that can give back a meaning to something very difficult to signify, start again a process of symbolic re-creation, as the foundations for the development of a new thought.

> Identifying with both the abuser and his victim is difficult. You are feeling both the guilt of the rapist and the shame of his victim. You are ashamed and you want to hide away. You feel powerless. And abused. For that reason, perhaps, you are angry with a person who suffered enormous wrongs in the past but could today become, in turn, an abuser. He keeps asking you for compensation, he has never enough.

Fornari (1981, 1988) added that this way of thinking was very close to the Greeks, who thought that evil was linked to Ananke, that evil was in the Ananke, as a destiny of nature inside which we are born. He said that our task was to take it upon ourselves … the poet takes it upon himself … the group, with the help of the poet, can take it upon itself…

> There are times when they may even thank you, if you confront them with what they did or what they suffered. Perhaps because they feel that you helped them look at the frightful things that have happened. You may think of taking a few steps forward whenever a confrontation is possible…

A family … help

A member of the group describes a drawing where he tried to show the situation of the group, as he is feeling it now: the middle part of his drawing is covered with lots of large circles, densely coloured in black and in red. 'I am in the picture', the group member tells us, 'and I am crossing all the circles. From the right to the left, towards the circles more thickly coloured in red. Then I turn and look back at my course. The picture is divided into two horizontal bands; in the lower part, circles with lots of small figures inside, in the upper part, circles with two large figures inside.'

The group suggests that the circles stand for the various stages the group went through; there is a lot of aggression of which the narrator is painfully aware. The new element is the red colour the narrator is heading towards; it represents passion, a feeling that seemed not yet acknowledged and that, with the group work, can rise to the surface.

Some more work on the description of the picture leads us to understand that the figures drawn on the lower part are as small as children!

Do they stand for the abused children the caregivers are involved with, for the caregivers themselves, needing help from the group and in the group, do they stand for us, the psychoanalysts, needing help for our own group?

The passion for our job allows us all to remain inside a violent, at times unbearable reality, without running away, physically or emotionally.

In the upper part of the picture there are two bigger figures, two adults: the leader of the psychoanalysts' group and a relative the group member is fond of.

We, the psychoanalysts, can really feel as fragile as children when we are dealing with the caregivers who help abused children. The passion for our job comes to our rescue, as well as the help of someone who can temporarily play the role of the supporting adult for us; this experience is familiar in our jobs and in our lives. However, we must look for it and find it each time, inside and outside us, to recover the possibility of not falling in the grip of the absence of thought and of loneliness, to expand our vision and regain our hopes.

> The child's need for a peculiar kind of receptiveness from the adult continues also during the second half of the child's first year of life. The child will have times of great fragility when he has reached several psychological stages. Even when the child has grown up, he will still have the recurring need for a more childish relationship with parents and with other adults. The need for someone to perform, although temporarily, the function of external mental container of our more upsetting feelings will recur in the course of our lives.
>
> (Judy Shuttleword, 1993, p. 41)

The group helps us think of anxiety ... it works as a string cradle and contains ...

The octopus group

Stairs, doors, halls and walls appear in the group. However, these borders do not seem to protect and create a place where you can also feel safe ... partitions/walls letting sounds and voices come through ... A member of the group begins to speak in a grey, sad, tired voice. Carrying on with the job is getting more and more difficult ... impossible. The organisation he belongs to seems to perform a mutilating function. His passion is fading as time goes by. He feels crushed by a machinery that paralyses his vital energy.

The group is frightened. The image of an octopus appears; another group member says: 'We all seem in the clutches of a giant octopus … what we complained of is true: red tape, competition, envy, destructiveness. However, we manage quite often to do something good and important in our job!' The group restarts. Each member tells his octopus story, the octopus dwindles as it goes from one member to the other, until it becomes a very small octopus that each of them can be responsible for: throw it back into the sea … fry it in the pan … (It is possible now to approach the idea that we are, sometimes, part of the octopus, that we were doubtless part of it, until this moment, in the here and now of the sitting.) The group finds again its competence at reliving a sustainable passion. In the following sitting the group member who had spoken about his inability to cope thanks the group.

The 'ceremonious' group

The group is meeting again for its second season; it is starting again after a year of work, later, however, than the previous year. It has changed, some members are missing and there are some new ones.

The introductions begin: a new member, smiling and mundane, addresses all the members … another member quickly takes his coat and wears it … shivering … the group is wondering: To show? Not to show? To give details of ourselves, our jobs, our qualifications?

An image of the previous year of work is evoked: 'Idle chitchat or toilet cleaning?'

The group is swinging. Another member begins to tell a terrible story: a little girl, living in a support community, stopped by a toy shop during a walk with her caregiver. She then acted out bewildering and explicit sexual proposals towards the caregiver. The girl has been sold to the best bidder for years; she has been a victim of repeated abuse and has learned to show off her beauty. To be chosen allowed her to survive.

The group begins to speak of its belated start, of their uncertainty, of their fears for its survival. The group was afraid it would die. It wondered whether it was liked enough. We feared that we could not choose, or choose again, one another.

The group can give a meaning to its ceremoniousness.

The gang group

The group is moving haphazardly: couples and subgroups appear. A new member, for whom the group has been waiting for a long time, is now here; he had serious difficulties twice before. The group had worked on its feelings of worry and anger about that in the previous sittings. A group member starts to speak: three brothers have arrived at the support community where he is working. Their previous structure is now hosting refugees, no longer minors.

The three children set up among themselves a way to cope with the difficulties of their life. The small gang tried, right from the start, to impose its own rules: for instance, they do not think it worthwhile to politely greet the headmistress. The community caregivers do not take action. The headmistress tries firmly to make them respect the rules that she believes are important: greet one another, follow the schedule ... The caregivers shut her out of their meetings. One of the brothers, the middle one, has a psychic illness, perhaps an acute psychotic episode. He is admitted to hospital. During his stay in hospital, the headmistress dismisses him from the community; the caregivers rise up, asking the headmistress to resign. They want another headmistress.

The group is in turmoil: several members speak in a disorderly way, on a personal level, about the situation, offering advice, reflections, previous experiences.

Interactions among members become excited, voices rise louder, violent and vulgar terms are thrown about. The possibility of thinking, to cope with the problems that the new member's arrival has created and is creating, is dismissed. The group as a place of reception no longer exists.

The 'headmistress': The thought, that can account for and bind together thoughts, feelings and emotions, both of the individuals and of the group, is dismissed in the here and now. It takes back its place at the end of the sitting, with this awareness.

In the following sitting the group reflects on its own and their individual limits and on the need to take them into account, to avoid mental pain.

Abused children, caregivers, psychoanalysts ... voices from the groups

At the beginning of these reflections I spoke of minds that are shutting off, and of the toil and work needed to prevent this from happening and to promote, instead, incessantly, possible new openings. The groups I dealt with seem to me the suitable setting for this job and this toil, and the voices we heard are speaking of just that: of the continuing and incessant efforts aimed at widening the feeling, against the continuing, simultaneous, systematic efforts aimed at restricting the individual and group minds.

We must deal all the time with stupidity (I am using here a word that seems to me synonymous to Brenman's concept of 'narrow-mindedness' that I mentioned at the beginning), in Bion's words, the manifestation of something obstructing the process of receiving things inside oneself (Bion, 1957), which provides the basis for communication. This obstruction is at times perceived in one voice, at times in another, at times in the group as a whole, at times it comes from some other place to hinder understanding.

We start our journey from a voice saying that nothing has happened, then we hear another, fearfully stating that, on the contrary, something very serious has happened and who caused it to happen said that nothing would happen. Yet another voice tells us again that what happened is very serious indeed, an unceasing dialogue with several voices, where, through many difficulties, the ability of the group to act as a container is outlined. Or rather, the specific containing quality of the group behaviour, that – containing – allows us to modify the experience, is outlined.

Acknowledgements

With thanks to A. Camisassi, S. Bomarsi, C. Napoli, E. A. Pellerano and I. Pozzoli.

References

Bion, W. R. (1957). La superbia. Translation in *Analisi degli Schizofrenici e metodo Psicoanalitico*. Rome: Armando, 1970.
Bion, W. R. (1961). *Esperienze nei gruppi*. Translation. Rome: Armando, 1971.
Bion, W. R. (1962a). Una teoria del pensiero. In *Analisi degli Schizofrenici e metodo psicoanalitico*. Rome: Armando, 1970.
Bion, W. R. (1962b). *Apprendere dall'esperienza*. Rome: Armando, 1972.
Bion, W. R. (1965). *Trasformazioni*. Rome: Armando, 1973.
Brecht, B. (2015). *Poesie Politiche*. Torino: Einaudi.
Brenman, E. (1995). Crudeltà e ristrettezza mentale in Melanie Klein e il suo impatto sulla Psicoanalisi oggi. Volume 1. La teoria. Rome: Astrolabio.
Fornari, F. (1981). *Simbolo e Codice. Dal processo psicoanalitico all'analisi istituzionale*. Milan: Feltrinelli.
Longo, M. & Neri, C. (1985). Il gruppo esperienziale nel Corso di Laurea in Psicologia. Riflessioni sul modello e la sua utilizzazione. In *Funzione analitica e formazione alla psicoterapia di gruppo*. Rome: Borla.
Neri, C. (1979a). La culla di spago. In *Quadrangolo, IV, 1*. Rome: Rivista di Psicoanalisi e Scienze Sociali.
Neri, C. (1979b). Rappresentazione, costruzione, interpretazione nel gruppo. In *Gruppo e funzione analitica*. Rome: CRPG.
Neri, C. (1979c). La torre di Babele. Lingua, appartenenza, spazio, tempo nello stato gruppale nascente. In *Gruppo e Funzione analitica*. Rome: CRPG.
Neri, C. (1982). Gruppo. Individuo, 1. In *Gruppo e funzione analitica*. Rome: CRPG.
Neri, C. (1983). Guppo. Individuo (oscillazioni e complementarità). In *Quaderni di Psicoterapia di gruppo*. Rome: Borla.
Neri, C. (2004). *Gruppo*. Rome: Borla.
Shuttleworth, J. (1993) Teoria Psicoanalitica e sviluppo infantile. In *Neonati visti da vicino L'Osservazione secondo il modello Tavistock*, Rome: Astrolabio.

14 What happens to pain

The evolution of the request

Elisa Alice Pellerano and Ivana Pozzoli

What happens to pain? The pain we experience during our jobs, besides the pain we experience during our lives? The violence, the abuse, the mistreatments, the losses, the mourning. Is it possible to deal with? To modify it and make it somehow thinkable? Or is it necessary to look for someone who shares it and is able to care for us, to avoid dragging it behind like a dead weight? Can the group be a useful tool in the management of deeply painful situations?

In 2014 a few members of the Genoese Centre of Psychoanalysis received a request for help from social and health workers; their job deals, in different ways and with different working abilities – both in the public and private sectors – with such themes as minor abuse and mistreatment. Twelve colleagues, both member and candidate psychoanalysts, met to set up a working group as an answer to their request. Our aims were thinking about the issue of violence and offering projects and actions to cope with it, starting from the premise that the group setting would be the most suitable tool.

The group, still in existence, is composed of members with different levels of experience and different roles within the local executive committee. You can ask for membership, prior assessment of the entry requests. We decided to appoint different posts, at the beginning through 'random choice': a leader and a secretary, both with a yearly mandate.

We hold monthly meetings; the idea is that taking up such an issue in a group can be the most enriching direct experience about the dynamics of violence. We look for ways to cope with and modify it, thanks to a sustainable cooperation among members.

At the time, we thought that answering the social and health workers' request was important and we offered them a place, i.e. a monthly, low-cost 'group', as an instrument of support and help. Some of us chose to propose the 'experience group', meaning what Neri (1985) defines as

> a group ... situation where, starting from the experience inside an analytically led group, the observation of transformative phenomena and factors that belong more properly to groups is central ... The aim is maintaining

the cooperation among members, to underline the cognitive function of the group.

(p. 171)

The groups are still in existence, under the care of the psychoanalysts who take part in the project. Their aim is to offer the experience of the group and of its analytic cognitive function as an instrument for the maintenance of one's own mind, severely tried by the constant contact with borderline situations: abuse and mistreatment, both between peers and between adults and minors.

In both the worker and the colleague group, we could realize how difficult it was to keep a steady course towards our working goals, especially when disturbing issues, such as hate, abuse and violence were affecting the emotions of the group members.

In the former group, the presence of a conductor, of a third party acknowledged as the leader, with a protective function, enabled us to work on what moved the group at the time of 'hic and nunc'.

In the group of the colleagues we had, perhaps inevitably, to cope with our own violence, due to the different setting; nobody was appointed 'super partes' to contain and explain it.

We tried to keep it in check and modify it, whenever it was possible. But often, in spite of all efforts, we surrendered and acted it out. A confirmation was that the fragile, or 'small' parts, present in anyone ended up being mistreated in the group. So we felt on our own skin the burning range of emotions caused by taking up the role of the victim, but also of the executioner: guilt, shame, humiliation, paranoia and rivalry.

Hence the wish to take part, also as colleagues, in a group training which could help us experience these issues, with the help of a supervisor appointed as the leader.

The colleague group has recently ended the first part of an experience group led by a trainer appointed outside the centre. It was a very enriching experience and during it – it took place in 2017 – the group seemed to be working very lively again. However, the situation was not resolved at the end of the training. The strain was back, even worse than before. Powerful but hidden conflicts, distrust and slander replaced the 'group work'. To say it with Bion, the emotions unacknowledged, in the absence of a leader appointed to recognise them, carried the group towards the risk of going off track, to the point that we asked ourselves whether going on still had any sense.

We questioned ourselves on what was happening. On the one hand, we think the difficulties and the confusion due to the issue we were dealing with were unavoidable; on the other, we suppose that the absence of an acknowledged leadership did not allow us to elaborate and overcome the impasse we were moored in.

The antidote, so to speak, could be to keep confronting oneself and others, as honestly as possible. Talking with colleagues, going on with one's own self-analysis and training and, above all, believing that working together can lead to a true acknowledgement of the experiences and responsibilities of each of us. Humbly accepting to hold both roles in the group, the victim and the executioner.

Does it mean that the only way to 'make use of indigestible pain' can be entering a dimension of honesty, acknowledging one's human fallibility and our continuous need for analysis, training and care?

The experience group of the social and health workers had no therapeutic goals, nor was there, at least at the beginning, a conscious need for 'the request to be cared for'. But the 'burning' and at times demanding experience of sharing such heavy issues in the group led to an evolution of the request.

Here starts our reflection, from the idea that sharing such disturbing issues in a group setting resulted in dealing with experienced, rather than told, situations. They were a sore trial for all members, even the better trained and equipped. We were trapped by the violence of what we were experiencing, for which we could not immediately find any meaning, to give us comfort; but we also felt the need to question ourselves. We felt the urge to flee, but also accepted to stay as long as needed, to share and try to understand. A dynamic, wild and at times brutal dimension, typical of groups, that we could live and afterwards think, not without difficulty, both among colleagues and with the social and health workers group. We acknowledged its complexity, but at the same time its potential richness. The wish to go on with a group training was rekindled among the colleagues who had worked on that; but, above all, the social and health workers group asked to be therapeutically taken in charge.

This is the third edition of the experience groups with social and health workers. Two psychoanalysts manage the groups: one as the leader and the other as a participating observer. Their main task is to promote the analytical function of the group, keeping a circular level of communication among members. The member number ranges from eight (minimum) to fourteen (maximum) participants for each group. The group work goes on for one year, with a fixed ending time, with ten monthly sittings, each of them lasting two hours. There is besides the possibility for members to renew their participation to the next edition of the group, from one year to the following, or instead to terminate their experience.

Even if the groups have a fixed ending time, their frequency and duration allow for an evolution of this experience. A group history and memory are structured, as well as a search for a common language.

The following material deals with the evolution of the request that we could observe, as leaders, in the experience group with the social and health workers. As if the group experience had led them to acknowledge their 'need for analysis and care' and to hope that the leaders would fulfil their wish. As a need to focus on their own pain, rather than on the users' pain. They hope to make use of their pain and to become better equipped to deal with the traumas they encounter during their lives and of their job.

Clinical vignette

This is the third meeting of the new edition of the experience group. Some of the members are by now old members, having attended for years, while others have just arrived. This creates a peculiar atmosphere developing along the adults–children dimension.

During the previous meeting we had spoken, touchingly, of the story of a baby girl who had died at seven months because her mother had stopped caring for her immediately after her birth.

The sitting opens with two apparently split positions. The members' attention is focused on the mistreatments often suffered by young children, inexperienced and needy. Inhuman professionals, who take advantage of the young, are present alongside mothers who murder their own children. The group seems to give voice to the death anxiety, vivid at that time, to the fear that something alive and newly born can be neglected and left to die, instead of being supported.

As an answer to that, other members stand up for the role of the parents who also, they remind the group, are sometimes murdered by their children.

Hate then seems to be the dominant emotion in the group, both from the parents-leaders towards the children-members, and from the latter as an answer to the murder of the need for attention, care and therapy in the children.

But the following speakers introduce a different point of view, trying to create a connection between the former two. The issue of maternity is taken up as a condition to support and protect. And a place, the Amaman (in Spanish: 'breastfed') where it can be cared for.

Agata adds that she watched a documentary about a mother who had murdered her child. She was stricken by the woman's humanity; instead of facing a monster, she had discovered a person. A desperate mother, who believed death would be the only solution for herself and for her child.

This is perhaps the first time, during our meetings, that a request for help is outlined although in the form of the need to be reassured. Humiliation as the only solution is contrasted by an idealised mother group to depend on. On the one hand, the group is asking for help, but on the other, fears the emancipating function that permits to acknowledge the pain and elaborate the mourning and proposes a sort of regressive protection based on the denial work.

As the leaders, we are stricken by the continuity with the issue raised in the previous meeting. As if the experience of a baby girl left to die and of a mother unable to realize the fact and care for her had seeped into each member. An experience that keeps coming back into the group as something intimate and personal. They speak of their lives with deep poignancy and involvement.

They seem to be telling us: 'We are suffering, not only the abused, mistreated children! We are suffering, why don't you care for us? Why don't you help us understand the reasons of a mother and those of a child?'

When we understand their real request for help, we can finally take up again the issue of group elaboration of despair. At this point Barbara wishes to tell us something very painful about herself, since now time and place allow her to distance herself from it. It is a hopeful story, too. Her grandmother was one of those women who tried to murder their children. Then she committed suicide. Both her children survived and one of them is her mother, who is a normal woman now. She adds ironically: 'Do not think that everything is all right. My mother had to slice her head away. She does not believe in the psychic part, and I am a psychologist. Then I look at my daughter and wonder what will happen when she has a child.' She seems to be telling us that some pain is so impossible to digest, that you need to slice it away in order to survive. Unless we try to understand something together, to prevent it from happening again. She is a strong woman, it is her recognized place in the group. That is why, maybe, she can afford to say so clearly and directly that we need help.

It is, however, a huge and demanding request, a heavy load thrown upon the leader. It is frightening, at first. So the leader recalls the story of a difficult patient of hers, towards whom she experiences very strong feelings of refusal. A suffering and very demanding mother: it is difficult to establish a connection and catch a glimpse of her fragility. She has recently lost her father, but cannot acknowledge the pain of her loss.

And here comes the mourning for the father, evoked by the leader as the alarming absence of a need that the group has denied for a long time: the possibility of a therapeutic third position. The leader must take upon herself the responsibility of dealing with the pain.

Now someone takes up the issue of how you can react to the suffering, the mourning and the losses. There is a woman, whose mother is suffering from Alzheimer's, who must go on 'running' to hold everything together. Sooner or later she is going to crash.

Giorgio tells us the meaning of living with an announced mourning, when, day after day, you see a person getting worse. He tells us the story of a patient of his who is dealing with the same situation. He hopes he can help him cope with it. Introducing the possibility of being helped can enable him to regard pain with deeper humanity. The patient of the leader becomes then a little girl compelled to behave as an adult, at only two years of age: she did not know how to play and only wanted to study. The group has introduced the issue of hope, that allows them to be heard in their needs and wishes.

The initial death anxiety, of a newborn baby at risk of being left alone to die, can now be reinterpreted as the fear that their request for help is not heard.

There is a patient, the group, who tells about his pain and his suffering for the loss. And there is someone who can help him. They are asking for help to understand themselves. Their suffering is actually their problem. They all are tempted to slice the head away, to avoid taking on the pain, to deny it and to reject who, on the contrary, is encouraging them to share it, as Barbara's mother had to do. However, a territory, a space for thought is rising in the group, something alive to take care of, something we need to work on, together with them, for a long time.

References

Neri, C., in collaboration with M. Longo and P. Cupelloni (1985). The 'Experience Group' in Degree Course in Psychology: Use of the Literary Texts. In *Analytic Function and Training for Group Psychotherapy*, ed. E. B. Croce. Rome: Borla, pp. 171–176.

15 The group is frightened and frightening

Chiara Napoli and Anna Maria Risso

The caregivers' group is meeting for the third year under the supervision of two psychoanalysts of the Genoese Centre of Psychoanalysis who play different roles in the group: a conductor and a participating observer.

There are seven members from the previous two years and four new members. Five members of the previous year's group are missing; three of them have explained the reasons why they are not carrying on with this experience. They discussed and worked through these reasons towards the end of the second year of group work.

During the first meeting, we announce that one of the two psychoanalysts (the participating observer) will not be able to attend the next two meetings. The group atmosphere is tense, anxious, worried; someone wonders and asks, 'Why?' Phantasies and anxieties about 'disappearances' begin to take shape. The psychoanalyst with the role of participating observer will be absent for the next two meetings: what is happening to this group?

'Where have we ended up?' A newcomer timidly tries to tell something about herself, introduces herself, asks some questions, 'I was wondering what I can bring in here. My most private emotions, too, can I tell you my story all the way?'

The group is frightened and frightening.

Where do our stories, secrets and confessions end up? The image of a group that swallows and dispatches them seems to take shape; perhaps it does the same to people, as well? We begin to reflect, painstakingly, on the 'disappearances', we repeat the missing persons' names, evoke their stories and revive the meetings when it happened. The group tries to remember and understand.

The conductor psychoanalyst remarks that the group is trying to piece their story together, revisit their grief, their errors, their losses.

The members of the previous years (all women) seem to be particularly sorry for the absence of a young colleague who had attended the previous groups and had so often told us about her very dramatic and deeply painful work events. During the last year, the young woman had attended the group with a male colleague she was working together with in the same unit. Together they had spoken about their extreme difficulties. During the last meetings, they had told us about their forthcoming layoff. The newcomers listen attentively to this story, one of the 'old ones' says, 'We are certainly not making a good impression: is the group of help?' Does it help? To be laid off?

A newcomer says, 'I am sorry that you lost your little sister.' At this point, one of the psychoanalysts (the participating observer), using the voice inflection customary for fairy tales, speaks about the bogeyman and the possibility that the bogeyman snatched their little sister away.

The two missing persons who did not account for their absence are the man and the woman who were working together; perhaps the little sister, who had attended the group for two years, would have liked to come again. Did the bogeyman prevent her? 'We are all women now,' somebody remarks. 'Then we are safe, for this year,' giggles somebody else. 'However, they have both lost their job, for sure, and yet they came here to learn how to do a better job.' Fear finds its way back into the group, which goes back to its inner persecutory aspect after a very brief stay in a reassuring and homogeneous group activity.

At the end of the meeting, one of the new members realises she is still wearing her coat and remarks, 'Unbuttoning is not easy.' Does the group help you in your life, or does it kill you? Have the weakest disappeared, or are they going to disappear? Certainly, in such a situation, eventually your turn is up. You must hide your secrets, your frailty, but also your personality, you must button up and try to blend with the others as far as possible.

The second meeting begins: the atmosphere is courteous, composed and pensive. Outside, in the square near the Psychoanalytic Centre of Genoa, a demonstration is in progress: we can hear shouts, cries, whistles and ambulance sirens. The group, however, seems to ignore the noise from outside, does not lose its composure. The psychoanalyst (conductor) who is present remarks on it. Is the group buttoned up, is it unable to take off its coat? What might we see under the coats?

After a long silence, Paola speaks, lively and emotionally, about one of her working experiences as a child neuropsychiatrist. She is temporarily sending away a teenage girl from her mother. The woman is going through a difficult period both in her personal and working life. She has separated from her husband and her parents – the girl's grandparents – cannot help her now. The social workers suggest the girl's placement in a residential childcare institution for a few months, with the possibility to spend her weekends at home. Paola describes joint talks, with both mother and grandmother, when the grandmother seems to be taking advantage of this opportunity to be cruel to her own daughter, so unfortunate – she lost her husband, her job. At the same time, the mother is aggressive to Paola, trying to control and channel her help directly, as if trusting somebody's competence were too difficult for her.

The narration is full of emotion and, while she is talking, Paola often indicates the empty chair of the absent psychoanalyst. The present psychoanalyst points it out to the group and wonders about the situation of the group now.

The group is turning a deaf ear to the violent event Paola is trying to make clear. The lack of one psychoanalyst leaves the other alone in a difficult working context; will she manage to deal with the needs of the group? The group is not helping her, hindered, in turn, by the absence; on the contrary, it could be aggressive and lose its ability to work. Paola claims her expertise and suggests using the group community.

The group communicates again. Why is the (participating observer) psychoanalyst absent? Can the psychoanalysts not get along with each other? Did they expel one of them? Why? Is a war between generations under way? (The psychoanalyst with the role of conductor is older than the psychoanalyst with the role of participating observer.) Who is caring for the group and its members?

We must find again a 'community' of intents. Is Paola suggesting just that? In that case, each role must be acknowledged. In the following meeting, one member will speak about a mother who, faced with her daughter's learning difficulties, becomes expulsive and cruel.

The phantasy of a group that cannot bear its members to express their difficulties returns powerfully, a group that expels those who mention them. A group that, acting this way, seems in turn to be suffering from a learning difficulty, that cannot learn how to work in a new way.

The fourth meeting begins with the roll call of the absent members: there are four. The psychoanalyst who was absent the previous two meetings is now back.

One member, Gloria, begins: I do not know if this is the right place to tell these things. However, I must lift a weight that has been a burden on me for some time now. I am going to retire in a year and I am the head of a centre dealing with short-term projects of psychiatric rehabilitation. Our users, only women so far, have always been rather self-sufficient and the programme prepared for each of them provided a stay of three months. The head physician changed a few months ago; he is young and with little community experience; after his mental hospital practice, he is not accustomed to getting his hands dirty. Due, I believe, just to economic reasons, he decided to change the type of users: he has admitted two men with low IQs. The IQ of the more intelligent is 64 ... I do not even want to know about the other. Two insane men, only waiting to be removed to an RSA (= nursing home) and end their days in bed. One of them is such a chain smoker that he has no blood flow left in one foot; they may have to amputate. I need to accept all this, but, one year from retirement, I cannot come to terms with it ... and I am angry, yes, I am very angry.

Conductor psychoanalyst: Meeting again is not easy, a longer time has gone by [the group is meeting after a month and a half, due to the Christmas holidays)], can we still work in the same way? Has anything changed? Did the group always have the same purpose? Very violent events took place; Gloria is speaking about blind violence, regardless of anything or anybody. Can the group still help her? The group, created for the very purpose of dealing with violence?

Francesca: I think that accepting that your projects are changed is very difficult. It upsets the meaning of the work you have been doing so far.

Gloria: Just so. I cannot stand just that.

Rita: [she has turned purple] I cannot contain the emotions I am feeling. Perhaps because I am not used to this job, to this group [Rita is the last member, this is her second meeting]. I am amazed at your language, I am not used to it ... we are speaking of two persons ... new persons who have just arrived.

Gloria: Sorry, I am furious; I do not usually speak like that. His name is Pietro, one of them is called Pietro.

Conductor psychoanalyst: Is the group perhaps rediscovering its reason for being, is it returning to the right place? Violence makes people disappear, it tears them apart: we were speaking about numbers: 64, feet, malfunctioning brains, we hold a name now: Pietro?

Gloria: Yes, of course they are persons. I was saying it good-naturedly, insane men! Quite the opposite, I even like them. The man called Pietro, with a 64 IQ, wanted, by all means, to make a good impression on me when we first met. Nevertheless, I cannot think that my work of 30 years is upset.

Camilla: I understand what you are saying. I have been working and carrying out a project for a long time in a centre; I discovered that a colleague of mine, who is also a cooperative member of the centre, while I am not, copied the project to apply it, exactly the same, somewhere else.

Participating observer psychoanalyst (who was absent in the previous two meetings): I believe that the group is also speaking about my being absent twice, and today I am back. I am a member of this community, I have responsibilities inside this group and I should take care of it. Instead, I went elsewhere, to do something else.

Conductor psychoanalyst: However, we are rediscovering some persons: Pietro, Carla [the second psychoanalyst].

Patrizia: As Carla was speaking, I recollected a dream I had last night: I saw a beautiful woman, heavily made up but her features were very good. As I approached her, I was wondering why she was so heavily made up. The closer I got, the more clearly I could see a scar framing her face, as if her face were split in half and the scar kept together something very fragile, something that a miracle was keeping together. I was horrified. She was so beautiful; I understood why she was wearing make-up, to hide her scar from sight.

Rita: Let us say these things to our faces, in the open, as the saying goes!

Deborah: I, too, am upset today. Before coming here, I discovered that the wife of a teacher of mine is dying of a degenerative disease. He has completely given up working, teaching as well, since her assistance is a priority. About Carla's absence, I do not recognise myself in the anger. We have already seen it in the other meetings, perhaps you [addressing Carla] missed a few pieces; I do not need to talk about it any further.

Conductor psychoanalyst: Are we dealing with an alarming degenerative disease that could stop the group, blocking its potential for teaching?

Participating observer psychoanalyst: That beautiful face ... something very beautiful ... was torn apart ... something very violent took place.

Paola: It reminded me of a face disfigured by acid.

Patrizia: We certainly spoke about Carla's absence in the previous meetings, but a part of myself, where there are no words, is very angry, feels mistreated, it is so angry that perhaps it could throw acid.

The conductor psychoanalyst remarks that four group members are absent today. Deborah observes that, actually, she is angry with one of the absent members, who had asked her to notify the group of her absence. The group begins to speak about absences, about how angry and lonely you can feel when somebody is absent, treated like a thing.

Gloria: Eine Sache ... as the Nazi said of the Jews. They were no longer people, just a thing.

The group continues to reflect on the persecutory aspect of the absence, on its being inescapable, an experience that is part of our life, on the possibility to deal with it by sharing it. In the last remark, Rita relates a talk she had with one of her patients, who is an addict: 'To any solution we find, he will always point out what is missing.'

The conductor psychoanalyst invites the group to reflect on the communication that seems to suggest a problem of addiction in the group, toxic addiction to our own experience of absence that seems to prevent a change; a kind of learning deficit, a degenerative disease of the group that has often been reported.

Patrizia brings another dream to the following meeting: she has gone to the moon and she is trying to hold two babies; one is very beautiful, chubby, well nourished, but she realises regretfully that the other is emaciated and suffering. We evoke the 'conquest' of the moon ... who knows if they really went there ... why they went there ... perhaps at the time it made sense, in the USA– USSR challenge ... Going to the moon is linked to the very beautiful woman in the previous dream ... The group, that could detect the false beauty of the face marred by a scar, now seems engaged into realising that a 'lunar' vision of themselves is no longer possible; they need to make contact with a suffering part.

The group speaks about the two psychoanalysts; when one of them was absent, they tried to keep them together, to preserve an image of fake beauty ('they are not two, with different roles, they are a single thing'). The result was monstrous, to say the least, and monsters are frightening: better be clear and speak about it. The group wonders about the roles of the two psychoanalysts; it is now clear that they hold different roles, one is the conductor psychoanalyst and the other is the participating observer. The conductor psychoanalyst holds the responsibility for the group; of course, if the conductor fails, then the group fails as well ... going to the moon seems to give no assurances, either; one of the babies is emaciated and malnourished.

Perhaps going to the moon is meaningless; there are two groups: one is well nourished and functioning, dreaming and working, the other, suffering and persecuted by a monstrous, undifferentiated couple. Looking closely at the two psychoanalysts, seeing their different functions is perhaps better. However, this exposes them to new anxieties ... the group becomes capable of learning, to learn that they can even die.

Would the monstrous and persecutory fusion (a source of sour, devastating anger) give way to the differences, to the persons, to their fallibility, their mortality, to a new, 'newborn' suffering?

Part III
Legal aspects
Task and role of the judiciary in child abuse

16 Protecting the child and assessing the evidence

Task and role of the judiciary in child abuse

Cristina Maggia

I will try to describe the different and parallel roles of the judicial authority in Italy in situations where children or minors are subjected to sexual abuse. It is a challenging task, but I will try and I trust you will forgive my oversimplifying to be understood by 'outsiders'.

It should first be mentioned that a judicial authority is in place, in charge of receiving complaints of criminal acts (and sexual abuse on children is a criminal act), of performing the necessary investigations to collect evidence in support of the charge in court and of carrying out the proceedings that will result in a sentence of imprisonment, or otherwise in acquittal.

Such a judicial authority, which we will call 'ordinary', is made up of a public prosecutor, a first-instance judge and an appeal court judge. Its primary job includes repression and punishment of the offenders. It works alongside and in parallel with another judicial authority, which we will call 'juvenile'. Its job is not so much to punish the offender as to protect and safeguard the young victims of abuse from a non-protective/inappropriate home environment, where the abusive conduct took place. Sometimes the juvenile judicial authority needs to defend the victims from a family unable to protect them from the abuses. Such home environment, if not appropriately treated, could repeat its mistakes and jeopardise the child's safety again.

This different judicial authority includes, in turn, a public prosecutor's office (the juvenile prosecutor's office, where I personally work) and a judging body (the juvenile court) that, entrusted with the matter by the juvenile prosecutor, decides whether and how to act to protect the minor concerned.

As you can imagine, there may be a variety of cases in life in which such acts come to the surface. Sexual abuse on children is reported to the public prosecutor's office and both the ordinary and the juvenile judicial authority. As far as teenager victims are concerned, confidential remarks are made to the girl or boyfriend, or to schoolmates or teachers, both verbally or through the contents of essays or drawings. Those are often the subject of the reports made to our offices, which need to be thoroughly analysed in terms of seriousness and truthfulness. For younger children, hints are often contained in drawings or stories they tell the people they trust. For example, if resident in a community, they may tell their caregivers stories about their past life, or speak to a grandmother, whose judgement they do not fear, or to their favourite teacher. The situation is much less severe and painful – and definitely easier to address – if abuse is performed by a stranger to the family, such as a neighbour, a sports coach, a baby sitter. In these cases, the rule is that the story is mostly told by the 'young victim' to the parents, provided that these offer protection and represent a reference point that the child may trust.

Hence, in these cases, it is much easier both to ascertain the truth in court and to implement treatments for the young victim, of which the parents themselves usually take charge within the framework of their care duties.

Sometimes the same parents may remove their child from disturbing relations, ensure assistance and support, including psychological, and/to make them feel their sympathy and solidarity.

If, on the other hand, the abuser is a family member who lives with the child (perhaps a parent), the situation is – as you may understand – much more complicated: judicial operators must have special sensibility and considerable skill. Let me tell you more about the two different and parallel way of roles.

The first: criminal proceedings

As mentioned, judicial actions according to Italian law basically provide for two approaches: the first is a criminal approach, and starts from the fact that sexual abuse on children is a serious crime. The focus is to ascertain the truth to support the charge against the abusers and collect such evidence as is required to obtain their conviction and, therefore, their punishment.

More specifically, the parties involved in this approach include

1 the police forces entrusted by the public prosecutor to perform in-depth investigations;
2 the public prosecutor in charge of the criminal action against the adult abuser that, once the investigation is completed and the necessary evidence is collected, will apply for indictment before the ordinary court; and
3 the judge, in charge of the defendant's conviction or acquittal, based on the evidence collected during the investigation.

Investigations of this kind of criminal act imply a completely different approach compared to investigations of other common offences (robbery, drug trafficking, bribery, etc.).

All the parties involved, including the judicial police, need to develop specific skills to operate in this particular field.

A psychologist should always attend the interviews with the victims, whose anxieties, fears, reluctance and possible inaccuracies connected with the memory's trauma, rather than with intrinsic non-reliability, should be thoroughly understood.

The witnesses' emotional reactions, their crying, their use of certain phrases or their overdetachment or apparent coolness, should be described in the records, in that these are psychological mechanisms they sometimes adopt to protect themselves from a mental discomfort that is too painful to put up with.

In short, the approaches, different from the usual ones, should be implemented to evaluate the reliability of witnesses in these proceedings, and are not always part of the skill set of a non-specialised policeman or judge.

Sometimes expertise is required to evaluate the victim's ability to testify, especially if this is very young.

This is why teams of 'specialised' judges from the public prosecutor's office have been set up in larger cities. These teams are almost solely in charge of investigations on crimes against 'weak people', including children, women, disabled people, elderly people and so on, not just in terms of sexual abuse, but also whenever the offender attempts to subjugate a fragile individual.

These public prosecutors are supported by police forces, also specialised, whose activity is limited to this sector and who have developed special awareness of the issue. At the same time, again in larger cities, exists a specialised court section. This means that the same section always takes care of the same kind of proceedings, and therefore develops considerable experience with respect to issues that imply being familiar with the mechanisms of the human mind.

Criticalities obviously include time and caution: a prompt assessment to the victim's story is key, even if not always exhaustive, particularly if the victim is a very young child, whose communication skills are not fully developed.

Certain ignominious charges need to be strongly supported by evidence to avoid creating non-existent 'monsters' and causing damage to people and to entire families.

To protect the victims and ensure the truthfulness of their story, an approach called 'pre-trial hearing' is used. This consists in having the abused minors, supported by a psychologist, tell their story before the judge. An adversarial process takes place, which means that the hearing is also attended by the public prosecutor, the defence attorney and the suspect, all located in different rooms divided by a mirrored glass, where they can participate – unseen by the witness – and ask questions only via the psychologist, who speaks directly to the child.

Once this process is completed, the young victim no longer needs to be heard, and the relevant records shall constitute the evidence used during the proceedings. This is a highly protective approach, which allows the collecting of evidence for good with all the guarantees offered by the adversarial process, without exposing the child to additional traumas deriving from repeated hearings and from the stress connected with the need to appear in the court room.

In our legal framework, in fact, criminal proceedings provide for balancing the victim's right to complain and obtain justice, with the right of any charged citizen to be tried in court and judged in compliance with the fundamental guarantees of defence, no matter how serious the criminal act claimed to have taken place.

The second: the juvenile proceedings for protection of the victim

At the same time, as mentioned, steps should be taken in some cases to provide protection to the abused child, particularly when the family seems to be or is the cause of the abuse. Or blamed for the emotional and material neglect that may have promoted the minor's encounter with his, or her, persecutor.

As mentioned, the juvenile judicial authority takes charge of this, sometimes even more promptly than the criminal proceedings against the abuser.

As a matter of fact, the elements required to ensure the child's protection are quicker to collect and less specific than those required to demonstrate the criminal liability of an individual, and therefore to obtain their conviction.

More specifically, a child's discomfort and pain can be demonstrated by several elements that need to be observed, evaluated and appreciated jointly, even if they are not proof of the crime's existence.

A parent's neglect, carelessness, non-affection, coolness, manipulation or pathological narcissism are no crimes and, as such, do not allow the demonstrating of the existence of a criminal conduct, but can certainly lead the juvenile judicial authority to remove the child from a family that takes such attitudes as a lifestyle, which we would all define as 'abusive', albeit not in a criminal sense.

This is why both judicial systems – parallel but having different purposes – need to be compared by the respective operators, in order to ensure that both goals are pursued.

Think about, for example, the quite frequent case of 'in-family abuse' performed by the mother's partner against the woman's teenager daughter: the girl was abused at home whenever she was left in the 'stepfather's' care – her mother being at work. After months of sexual abuse, the girl talked to a schoolmate, telling her about her powerlessness and anguish, specifying that she had tried to inform her mother about what was going on at home, while she was at work. Unfortunately, contrary to her expectations, she was not believed, but rather blamed by her mother for trying to provoke and 'seduce' with her youth her valuable partner – not least valuable because he paid the rent and part of the household expenses. The girl's loneliness was therefore boundless, as her anguish, until she managed to talk to her schoolmate, who encouraged her to tell her story to a teacher who promptly reported it to the authorities.

The report should be made first to the ordinary public prosecutor's office to initiate the criminal proceedings against the adult, then to the juvenile prosecutor's office to implement measures to protect the victim, whose mother, in charge of parental liability, was neither protective nor safeguarding, but rather an ally of the alleged abuser. Two opposite needs clashed here, though: on one hand, the girl should be promptly moved away from home, to remove her, as soon as possible, from a negative and harmful influence and from possible additional abuse; on the other, the only available proof was the victim's story, which was hardly confirmed. This therefore called for additional investigations (video surveillance) that, however, made it necessary for the girl to stay home somewhat longer.

The prompt intervention of the juvenile prosecutor's office, requesting and obtaining from the juvenile court that the victim can be removed from home, is appreciated and shared, but may also ban the collection of additional proof. This should be useful to demonstrate the guilt of the abuser and, if insufficient, to cause his acquittal, in this last case with all the additional severe consequences for the girl, treated as a slanderer by her family.

Therefore each time, in each case, being aware of the importance of both goals, the operators in charge of the criminal proceedings and those in charge of protecting the minor should always confront each other and work jointly. Only by talking to each other, by evaluating the specificities of each individual situation concerned and the need for more evidence or protection in each specific case can they achieve a win-win result, which involves both punishment and conviction, as well as protection.

Then, once the child is removed from the harmful family context, and evidence is collected in a pre-trial hearing, the young victim can start going through the facts towards recovery, supported by a psychotherapy that the state should provide. Unfortunately, the care and recovery process is often poor, due to a severe shortage of means and operators of public healthcare service staff. And things do not seem bound to improve.

One key issue of both the ordinary and the juvenile judicial authority is the ability to understand, or sometimes even just to 'feel or sense', when the reported sexual abuse is fake and instrumental. The most frequent case concerns one parent charging the other with sexual abuse on their child, during a conflicting separation process. In these cases, parents with highly narcissistic personalities, unable to bear the frustration of separation, seem willing to get revenge on their former partners by manipulating their child, to the point of contriving a fake sexual abuse by the other parent. The fact is reported and the allegations are repeated at all stages, in front of the police, in front of the prosecutor and the judge.

Children, aligned with the parent they perceive as the strongest and whom they are psychologically dependent on, often endure their parent's pressures and are convinced about non-existent facts. Often, they report to the investigators false stories only to make their mother, with whom their bond is quite strong, happy.

The specialised skills of public prosecutors and of the police forces, also supported by consultants, lead first to suspect, then to ascertain the falseness of such complaints. They can understand the danger posed by some parents, who are prepared to crush their children to take revenge for being betrayed and abandoned.

Without specialised operators, who can do a close check of the story, without prompt child separation from the pathological parent, non-existent monsters can be created, and barriers and breaks can occur between the child and the slandered parent that will not mend.

Significantly, such circumstances may arouse emotions, identification processes, unconscious mechanisms of escape from reality in each operator – whether a judge, a policeman or a lawyer. Such circumstances may be painful for the operators because they affect the myth of the family, seen as a 'haven of joy and comfort'.

The risk for the operator is to escape such pain through oversimplification, using stereotypes, without considering each individual background experience, that should be well known. The absence of specialised skills and the inability to take a highly critical vision of all such cases may generate additional anguish to the parties involved rather than lead to beneficial results.

I'll close with the comment that a poor action – even if taken with the best of intentions – may turn out to be some form of additional violence against the victim.

The child must be protected against every form of exploitation.

The author of this chapter was asked for further details of the references and this is her reply (see more in Chapter 13):

> I chose to turn the passages in question into the indirect speech. The concepts I was referring to have been published in different texts in the course of the years, rehashed, translated repeatedly ... I added the page numbers only in two points where there are just two texts to refer to. I added a reference. I had probably inserted arbitrary inverted commas in the graphic editing, I apologise for the inaccuracy. In two instances I could add no reference, since it is clinical material of the group in question ... the sentences in italics are actually the members' words.

Index

abuse: violence, distinction 78; *see also* child abuse; verbal abuse
Abuse and Ill-Treatment Group (Genoa) 91–8; aim 93; anxiety-provoking issues 93; Maria Pia Conte 91–2, 93; members 93; Stefano Bomarsi 92; violence and gender sub-groups 94–7
The Alien, Hering on 19
Alvarez, A. 12, 39, 53, 54, 56
Amaltea network (Genoa) 108
Ananke, and evil 114
animal cruelty 14
Anna Freud Institute 43, 48n3
Aulagnier, P. 26, 79
Australia, Child Abuse Commission 5
autonomy, as amputation 22–3

Balint, M., trauma theory 25
Bentovim, A., on 'Trauma Organised system' 50–1
Bion, W.: on child's recurring need 9–10, 115; on groups 110; on nightmares 108; theory of negative links 63
body, investing with meaning 10–11
body/mind, development 9
Bomarsi, S., Abuse and Ill-Treatment Group 92
Bowlby, J., child development 25
BPA (British Psychoanalytical Society) 1
breakdown, fear of 76
Brecht, B., *To the wavering* 113–14
Brenman Pick, I. 3
British Psychoanalytical Society 1
burn out, caregivers group 5, 115–16

Cabré, L. J. M. 3, 59
capacity development 34

caregivers: delusional expectations 101; effects of working with violence 104; narcissism 103; supporting adult, need for 115; and trauma 100, 101–2; working network, need for 102
caregivers group: burn out 5, 115–16; ceremoniousness 116; conductor psychoanalyst 124, 125, 127, 128; as container 118; defence mechanisms 105; dilapidation, fear of 113; 'disappearances' 124–5; drawing, interpretation 114–15; dreams 102, 105–6, 108–9, 112–13, 128; formation 104, 119; and gang group 116–17; Genoese Centre of Psychoanalysis 104; group and individuals, interaction 111; integrity of self 106–7; mental integrity 107; octopus story 116; participating observer psychoanalyst, absence 124, 125–6; poetic feelings 113–14; procedures 120; programme 119–20; psychosomatic symptoms 105; sharing of experiences 105; as 'stone grinders' 105; temporary nature of 112; therapeutic function 109; vaccine therapy 110; violence, discussion 126–7
castration fears, intergenerational transmission of 34–5
cats, as attachment figures 31
CEDAW (Convention on Elimination of All Forms of Discrimination against Women) 91
ceremoniousness, caregivers group 116
child: needs, Klein on 9; and play 67; recurring need 9–10, 115; *see also* unwelcome child

Index

child abuse: by grandfather 60–1; 'Christian's story' 13–14; and contact 9, 18; and damage to the self 10; false allegation 52–3; 'Giorgio's' story 59–64; international awareness of 2; overlooking of 12; psychoanalytic ideas 2; recovery from 56; representations 62; 'Sam's story' 14–16; vignettes 13–16; *see also* child abuse by child; child sexual abuse
child abuse by child 50; clinical narrative 51–7; 'Marco's' story 64–6
child abuser 63
child development, Bowlby 25
child sexual abuse: criminal proceedings 132–3; in the family 134; judiciary role in 131–6; and loss of childhood 11; and mental illness 12, 14–16; public prosecutor's role 131; and threat fantasies 19–20; victim protection 134–6
childhood, loss of, and child sexual abuse 11
children: maltreatment of 11–13; neglected 38
communication, pre-natal 96
'confusion of tongues' 3–4, 22, 24
contact, and child abuse 9, 18
Conte, M. P., Abuse and Ill-Treatment Group 91–2, 93
countertransference 31, 34–5, 63, 64, 65; reactions 3, 44; *see also* transference
COWAP (Committee of Woman and Psychoanalysis), conference 1
crisis interventions, STEP-BY-STEP refugee project 45
crypt creation, and trauma 82

Davies, J.M. & Frawley, M.G. 10
death, and loss of sense of time 23–4
del Favero, C. 99
displacement technique 55
dissociation, as means of survival 10
dreams, caregivers group 102, 105–6, 108–9, 112–13

eczema, and non-maternal containment 34
the ego: representational 79; splitting of 22; and trauma 22
enactment 31, 62
Eritrean community, Frankfurt 43
evil, and Ananke 114

family, child sexual abuse 134
FATRA (Counselling Center for Refugees and Victims of Torture) 41

Ferenczi, S. 3; *Confusion of tongues* 22; *On the Revision of the Interpretation of Dreams* 23; *The Clinical Diary* 23, 25; *The Unwelcome Child and His Death Instinct* 70; trauma theory 22, 23, 24, 25
FIRST STEPS groups: for mothers with babies/infants 45; for pregnant women 45
FIRST STEPS project 48n3
flight impulse, and trauma 41
forensic psychotherapy 53
forgetting, theory of 12
Fornari, F. 114
Foucault, M. 92
Frankfurt, Eritrean community 43
Freud, A. 38; *see also* Anna Freud Institute
Freud, S.: *Inhibitions, Symptoms and Anxiety* 69; on trauma 69; *see also* Sigmund Freud Institute
'frozen child' 63

Genoese Centre of Psychoanalysis 91, 99, 108; caregivers group 104, 119; *see also* Abuse and Ill-Treatment Group (Genoa)
Germany, refugee crisis 40
Glasser, M. 53
groups: Bion on 110; string cradle imagery 110; *see also* caregivers group

hair pulling 28; reasons for 33–4, 36, 38
Hering, C., on *The Alien* 19

IDeA Centre 43, 48fn2
insecurity, and perfectionism 33
IPA (International Psychoanalytical Association) 1; inter-committee on child abuse 4
Istanbul Convention (2011) 91

judiciary: role in child sexual abuse 131–6; structure 131

Klein, M.: on child's needs 9; on trauma 24

Lacan, J. 24; on language 78–9
language, Lacan on 78–9
Laplanche, J. 79
Leuzinger-Bohleber, M. 4

Mann, M. 4
Manne, A., *Rape among the lamingtons* 5
'Medea fantasy' 45
mental illness, and child sexual abuse 12, 14–16

Michaelisdorf (Germany) refugee village 40; staff supervision 44–5
mind, birth of, and mother-child relationship 9
Moss, D. 18
mother-child relationship: and birth of the mind 9; early session 35–6; later session 37–9; 'Marco's' story 66; 'Todd's' story 28–39

narcissism 67; caregivers 103; pathological 134; and trauma 69
negative links, Bion's theory 63
Neri, C. 119
nightmares 60; Bion on 108

object relations theory 24–5, 70
Oedipus Complex 24, 67
Other, as containing object 19

paranoid phantasies 45
Parsons, M. 53, 54
perfectionism, and insecurity 33
Perini, M. 93
perversions 63–4
play, and the child 67
prison psychiatry 92
Project Arianna (Genoa) 108
psyche, self-defence 23
psychic destructiveness 71, 75
psychoanalysis, need for 26
psychoanalytic theory 22, 26
psychosis, infantile 13
Punch, the King, and the Queen play 55–6

refugee crisis, Germany 40
refugees: attacks on 40–1; traumatised 4, 41–5
relationship, and trauma 24
relative trauma, Winnicott 25
representations, of child abuse 62
repressed anger 28, 29–30
revenge phantasies 32
Rhodes, J., *Instrumental* 13
Rizzitelli, R. 99

Sala, J. 3, 4, 18, 19
schizophrenia, example 13–14, 20
scotomization, of trauma 101
seduction 11, 22; by child 64; and trauma 24
self, damage to, and child abuse 10
self-harming 28
sexual identity 31

SFI (Sigmund-Freud-Institute) 4, 40; work with traumatised refugees 41–3
Shengold, L. 9
Sigmund Freud Institute 4
silence, as violence 68
Skelton, R. 11
social and health workers group, experience group 119, 121–3
'soul murder' syndrome 9
splitting: and 'death' 23; of the ego 22
STEP-BY-STEP refugee project 40, 41, 43–7; adult evening programmes 47; concepts 43–4; crisis interventions 45; FIRST STEPS groups for mothers with babies/infants 45; FIRST STEPS groups for pregnant women 45; and integration 43; language courses 47; Michaelis Village 43; psychoanalytic assessments 45; psychoanalytic Children's painting group 46; psychoanalytic groups for adolescents 46; psychoanalytic modules 44–7; staff supervision at Michaelsdorf 44–5
stigmata 75
superego: conflict 32; development 34
survival guilt 43

therapist, as abuser 54
time, loss of sense of, and death 23–4
Tognoli Pasquali, L. 4; commentary on 'Marco's' story 66–8
transference 4, 30, 64, 66; depression 71; passion 71; *see also* countertransference
trauma 12; and caregivers 100, 101–2; constructive 25; and crypt creation 82; definition 47fn1; and the ego 22; and flight impulse 41; Freudian 24, 69; infantile 22; Klein on 24; latent 76; and narcissism 69; positive and negative 25; pre-oedipal stage 27n4; pre-verbal period 76; primary 69; refugees 4, 41–5; and relationship 24; 'retrospective' 25; scotomization of 101; and 'screen memories' 25; and seduction 24; shock and strain types, distinction 25; vicissitudes 71, 76; *see also* relative trauma
trauma theory: Balint 25; Ferenczi 22, 23, 24, 25
Trowell, J. 56

unwelcome child 4, 38, 70–1; in adulthood 70; 'Paola's' story 72–5; sense of non-existence 70, 73, 74, 75

verbal abuse 78; vignettes 80–1, 83–4, 85–7
victim protection, child sexual abuse 134–6
Vigna Tagliati, M. 4
violence: abuse, distinction 78; against women 91; discussion in caregivers group 126–7; effects on caregivers 104; of maternal interpretation 79; silence as 68; *The White Ribbon* (film) 101

Winnicott, D.W. 38, 50, 70, 71; *Fear of Breakdown* 76; relative trauma 25
women, violence against 91
Woods, J. 4

Zontini, G. 4